TRACY PORTER'S 74-YARD INTERCEPTION RETURN FOR A TOUCHDOWN WAS ALSO A DASH INTO HISTORY FOR THE SAINTS AND THEIR FANS AS THEY WON SUPER BOWL XLIV.

This book is available in quantity at special discounts for your group or organization.
For further information contact:

Triumph Books
542 South Dearborn Street
Suite 750
Chicago, IL 60605
Phone: (312) 939-3330
Fax: (312) 663-3557
www.triumphbooks.com

Printed in the United States of America
ISBN: 978-1-60078-496-5

All photographs courtesy of AP Images except where otherwise noted.
Front cover image courtesy of Getty Images.

Content packaged by Mojo Media, Inc.
Joe Funk: Editor
Jason Hinman: Creative Director

MARCHING IN

THE WORLD CHAMPION NEW ORLEANS SAINTS

CREG STEPHENSON

TRIUMPH
BOOKS

CONTENTS

INTRODUCTION

A FEELING 43 YEARS IN THE MAKING

If you listen closely, you can probably still hear the echoes of "Who Dat!?!" ringing down Bourbon Street, across Lake Ponchartrain, and throughout New Orleans Saints country. A city and a region that already knew how to party now have a reason to take it to another level. After more than four decades as the NFL's laughingstock, the Saints are Super Bowl champions.

It didn't come easy, though. The Saints' 31–17 victory over the Indianapolis Colts in Miami was the end of a wild ride that saw New Orleans burst out to a 13–0 record in 2009, only to lose their momentum in the final three regular-season games and stumble into the postseason.

The Saints found their identity again in the playoffs, blitzing past Arizona in the divisional round before knocking off Minnesota in one of the all-time classic NFC Championship Games. Then New Orleans rallied from a 10–0 deficit in Super Bowl XLIV, finally putting Peyton Manning and the Colts away with a dominant fourth-quarter effort.

It's difficult to think of the Saints' championship without considering what it means to the city of New Orleans and the Gulf Coast region, devastated as it was a little more than four years ago by Hurricane Katrina. The recovery and rebirth of New Orleans was certainly on the mind of the Super Bowl Most Valuable Player, a man who joined them team just months after the greatest natural disaster in American history.

"Four years ago, who ever thought this would happen?" quarterback Drew Brees said. "Eighty-five percent of the city was under water, all the residents evacuated all over the country, people never knowing if they were coming back or if New Orleans would come back. But not only the city came back, and the team came back…when the players got there, we all looked at one another and said, 'We're going to rebuild together.'

"We leaned on each other. This is the culmination of that."

The title run began in the heat and humidity of summertime, when the Saints set out to prove they were more than just a basketball-on-turf team that tried to beat its opponents by merely outscoring them. Sure, Brees, Reggie Bush, Marques Colston, and the core of the league's top offense were back, but it would be an oft-burned defense that would have to step forward if New Orleans was to become a true championship contender.

Newcomers such as Darren Sharper and Jabari Greer joined forces with holdovers such as Jonathan Vilma, Will Smith, and Roman Harper to forge one of the more opportunistic defensive units in the league, the brainchild of first-year coordinator Gregg Williams. And in the end, it would be one of those defensive players—a second-year man from Port Allen, Louisiana, by way of Indiana University—who would make the season's defining play and clinch the franchise's first championship in 43 seasons of existence.

Even without a championship, this season and postseason would have gone down as the greatest in team history. But by hoisting the Vince Lombardi Trophy as Super Bowl champions, the 2009 New Orleans Saints found a place among the greatest NFL stories ever told. ❦

OWNER TOM BENSON CELEBRATES WITH FANS AFTER THE GAME.

SUPER SAINTS!

SAINTS 31, COLTS 17 • SUPER BOWL XLIV • FEBRUARY 7, 2009 • SUN LIFE STADIUM, MIAMI GARDENS, FLORIDA

It was often said during the 2009 season that the New Orleans Saints would go only as far as Drew Brees and their opportunistic defense would carry them. As it turns out, that was all the way to a Super Bowl championship.

Brees passed for 288 yards and two touchdowns to give the Saints the lead, and cornerback Tracy Porter returned an interception 74 yards for a score to preserve it in New Orleans' 31–17 victory over the Indianapolis Colts in Super Bowl XLIV. The championship is the Saints' first since their inception in 1967, ending 43 years of misery for what was long considered the most downtrodden franchise in the NFL.

"I'm just proud of these players," coach Sean Payton said. "And I'm so happy for all our fans who have been so patient. It wasn't perfect, and yet they hung in there. In the second half, we played a lot better.… It was a great team win."

Coming off a thrilling overtime victory against Minnesota in the NFC Championship Game, New Orleans entered Super Bowl week in Miami as a consensus underdog to the Colts. Indianapolis had not only been there, done that as champions of Super Bowl XLI (also held in Miami), but featured quarterback Peyton Manning playing at the top of his game.

Manning had embarrassed the New York Jets' top-ranked defense in the AFC Championship Game, erasing an early deficit with a near-flawless passing performance. Against a Saints defense that was among the most-porous in the league—one that had given up nearly 500 yards in the victory over Minnesota—it only stood to reason Manning would pass the Colts to victory once again and secure his legacy as arguably the greatest quarterback of his generation.

For a quarter or more of Super Bowl XLIV, it appeared the pundits were correct. Indianapolis steamed out to a 10–0 lead, while New Orleans was having trouble piecing together any sort of offensive threat.

New Orleans went three-and-out on the game's opening possession and Manning went right to work out of Indianapolis' no-huddle offense. He moved the Colts as far as the Saints' 20, but a third-down pass fell incomplete and Indy had to settle for Matt Stover's 38-yard field goal and a 3–0 lead with 7:29 to play in the first quarter.

The Saints did manage one first down on their next possession, but ended up punting again. This time, Manning and company made them pay in a big way.

Joseph Addai ran for 53 yards on three carries during an 11-play, 96-yard drive, the longest in Super Bowl history. Manning hit Pierre Garcon for the touchdown, a beautiful 19-yard strike over the head of cornerback

DREW BREES FOUND MARQUES COLSTON SEVEN TIMES IN THE GAME FOR 83 YARDS TO LEAD ALL SAINTS RECEIVERS.

Usama Young, who moments earlier had replaced an injured Jabari Greer in the lineup (Greer would eventually return). With 36 seconds left in the first quarter, the Colts led 10–0.

The Saints finally got their feet under them as the second quarter began, driving as far as the Colts' 22-yard line before Brees was sacked by Dwight Freeney on third down. That brought on Garrett Hartley for a 46-yard field goal, cutting the deficit to 10–3 with 9:34 to play before halftime.

New Orleans got a key break on Indy's next possession, when Garcon dropped a wide- open third-down pass from Manning. That gave the Saints the ball back down by only one score, and Brees quickly moved them in position to tie the game.

A 27-yard pass to Marques Colston put the ball on the Colts' 3, and two plays moved New Orleans to the 1. But Indianapolis came up with back-to-back stops, first when Mike Bell slipped on third down and then when three defenders stuffed Pierre Thomas in the backfield on fourth down to give the Colts the ball back with less than two minutes to go before the break.

The Saints' defense stood tall, however, and forced a three-and-out. A 19-yard pass to Devery Henderson put New Orleans in field goal position again, and Hartley nailed a 44-yarder as time expired to make it 10–6 at intermission.

It was during halftime that Payton let his team in on a little secret–the Saints would attempt an onside kick to start the second half, choosing to try and get the ball back rather than turn it over to the red-hot Manning.

"We were really excited when he made the call," said linebacker Jonathan Casillas, a member of the Saints' kickoff team. "That changed everything."

Did it ever. Kickoff man Thomas Morstead bounced a perfect onside kick, and reserve safety Chris Reis jumped on the ball, then held on for dear life at the bottom of the pile. After a scrum for possession that

GARRETT HARTLEY, SHOWN HERE BEING CONGRATULATED BY TEAMMATE JAHRI EVANS, KEPT THE SAINTS CLOSE IN THE SECOND QUARTER WITH 46- AND 44-YARD FIELD GOALS.

PIERRE THOMAS DIVES
INTO THE END ZONE
AFTER A SHORT PASS
RECEPTION FROM BREES.
BACK JUDGE GREG STEED
IS ABOUT TO SIGNAL
THE SCORE.

took more than a minute to sort out, Reis emerged clutching the pigskin, and the Saints' offense took the field with all the momentum behind them.

It took just six plays to move the 59 yards for the touchdown, with Thomas hauling in Brees' screen pass and zig-zagging through the Colts' defense for a 16-yard score and New Orleans' first lead at 13–10 following Hartley's extra point. But it all started with the perfectly executed onside kick, which Payton had been cultivating all week.

"We talked about it during the week, and we had seen a couple of looks we felt pretty good about," Payton said. "At halftime, we told those guys, 'We're going to steal a possession here if we can.' Those guys executed and did a great job."

Manning was not to be outdone, however. He moved the Colts down the field to reclaim the lead, converting a pair of third downs before Addai's four-yard touchdown run made it 17–13 with 6:15 left in the third.

New Orleans pulled back within one at 17–16 on Hartley's 47-yard field goal with 2:01 remaining in the quarter, his Super Bowl-record third field goal of more than 40 yards in the game. That score would stand up into the fourth quarter, when the Saints would finally prove their championship mettle.

(OPPOSITE) JEREMY SHOCKEY CELEBRATES WITH TEAMMATES JONATHAN STINCHCOMB (78), JAHRI EVANS (73), AND JONATHAN GOODWIN (76) AFTER SCORING A TWO-YARD TOUCHDOWN IN THE SECOND HALF. (ABOVE) PEYTON MANNING AND THE COLTS COULD ONLY WATCH FROM THE SIDELINE AS THE SAINTS MOUNTED THEIR COMEBACK IN THE SECOND HALF.

Following Hartley's field goal, Manning and the Colts moved quickly into Saints territory, but could get no closer than the 33. Saints linebacker Jonathan Vilma had perfect coverage on a third-down incompletion to Austin Collie, then Stover missed wide left on a 51-yard field-goal attempt.

A 12-yard run by Reggie Bush and six consecutive completions by Brees put the ball inside the Colts' 10, and this time New Orleans punched it in. Thomas ran for three yards to the 2, then Brees hit Jeremy Shockey for the touchdown. Moments later, he connected with Lance Moore on a 2-point conversion—which was originally ruled incomplete but overturned by instant replay review—to put the Saints up by a touchdown, 24–17 with 5:42 to play.

But that was still plenty of time for the Colts, especially with Manning under center. Indy quickly got three first downs before being faced with third-and-5 on the New Orleans 31. That was when Manning made his fatal mistake. He looked for Reggie Wayne

(OPPOSITE) JONATHAN VILMA, WHO LED THE TEAM WITH SEVEN TACKLES ON THE DAY, AND BOBBY McCRAY TACKLE COLTS WIDEOUT PIERRE GARCON. (ABOVE) PETE TOWNSHEND AND THE WHO HEADLINED A MEMORABLE HALFTIME SHOW.

REGGIE BUSH BREAKS
FREE OF LINEBACKER GARY
BRACKETT (58) ON ONE
OF HIS FIVE CARRIES FOR
25 YARDS. BUSH ALSO
HAD FOUR CATCHES FOR
38 YARDS.

on a curl pattern to the left side, but Porter jumped the route and gathered in the interception, racing untouched 74 yards for the score and a 14-point Saints lead with 3:12 left in the game.

"It was great film study," Porter said. "We knew that on third-and-short they stack, and they like the outside release for the slant."

Said Manning, who threw for 333 yards and a touchdown in the game, "Made a great play. Made a great play. Corner made a heck of a play."

Nevertheless, Indianapolis still had time to mount a comeback, and Manning drove the Colts as far as the New Orleans 3. But his fourth-down pass fell incomplete in the end zone with 44 seconds to play, meaning all that was left was for Brees to kneel the ball to kill the clock and for the Saints to celebrate their Super Bowl championship.

In the moments after the game, Brees reflected on the journey taken by the team and its hometown during the season and the past several years. The one-time San Diego Charger has grown to embrace Who Dat Nation as much as it has embraced him since he joined the team in 2006. "We just believed in ourselves, and we knew that we had an entire city and maybe an entire country behind us," said Brees, named Super Bowl MVP for his 32-for-39 passing performance. "What can I say? I tried to imagine what this moment would be like for a long time, and it's better than expected.

"I'm just feeling like it was all meant to be. What can I say?"

Nothing needed to be said. The actions of Brees and company had spoken loudly enough. ෴

NEW ORLEANS SAINTS VS. INDIANAPOLIS COLTS						
	1	2	3	4	FINAL	
New Orleans	0	6	10	15	31	Record: (16–3)
Indianapolis	10	0	7	0	17	Record: (16–3)

UNHERALDED SAFETY CHRIS REIS (39) MADE HIMSELF A SAINTS LEGEND FOR LIFE AFTER RECOVERING AN ONSIDE KICK TO START THE SECOND HALF.

REGGIE BUSH HELPS GET THE PARTY STARTED WITH SAINTS FANS AFTER A WIN THAT IS SURE TO BE CELEBRATED FOR A LONG TIME ON BOURBON STREET.

SAINTS HISTORY:
A 43-YEAR MARCH TO GLORY

To understand the jubilation being displayed throughout the Gulf South for the New Orleans Saints' first-ever Super Bowl title, one need only look from where the franchise and city came. The Saints' NFL championship is the culmination of 43 years of the team's players, executives, and fans hoping against hope, dreaming the impossible dream, and wondering if their day would ever come.

That day is finally here, and it's much sweeter for "Who Dat" Nation considering all the franchise has been through since its inception. As recently as just last year, winning the Super Bowl remained seemingly outside the realm of possibility for a team that had advanced as far as a second playoff game only twice before 2009.

For their first 10 seconds at least, the New Orleans Saints were the greatest team in the history of professional football. In the Saints' first-ever game, September 17, 1967, against the Los Angeles Rams at Tulane Stadium, John Gilliam ran the opening kickoff back 94 yards for a touchdown.

But to say the team was unable to sustain that early momentum would be among the all-time great understatements. The Saints lost that first game to the Rams 27–13, which is fitting, because it is losing that would define the franchise for its first two decades.

Founded on All Saints Day 1966 and bankrolled by the fortune of Texas oilman John Mecom Jr., there were few highlight and even fewer victories for the New Orleans team in those early days. The Saints went a combined 14–40–2 in their first four years of existence, with the high point coming on November 8, 1970, with Tom Dempsey's NFL record 63-yard, game-winning field goal against the Detroit Lions.

The 1971 season marked a new era for New Orleans football, with the arrival of the team's first-round draft pick and eventual face of the franchise, quarterback Archie Manning. The team's fortunes would not improve drastically during the former Ole Miss star's 11-year career with the Saints (which saw the opening of the Louisiana Superdome in 1975), as New Orleans never finished better than 8–8 before Manning was traded to the Houston Oilers in 1982.

The 1980 season was the absolute nadir of New Orleans football, as the Saints went a league-worst 1–15. During the latter stages of that forgettable year, Saints fans began donning paper bags over their heads and referring to the team as the "Aints."

New Orleans remained outside of playoff contention for the first half of the 1980s, but things began

VINCE BUCK CELEBRATES A FUMBLE RECOVERY DURING A RARE POSITIVE SEASON IN SAINTS HISTORY. MOST OF THE 1991 SQUAD HAD BEEN TO THE PLAYOFFS THE YEAR BEFORE, BUT IT WAS THEIR DIVISION-WINNING TEAM THAT LEFT OWNER TOM BENSON MEMORABLY DANCING ON THE SIDELINES.

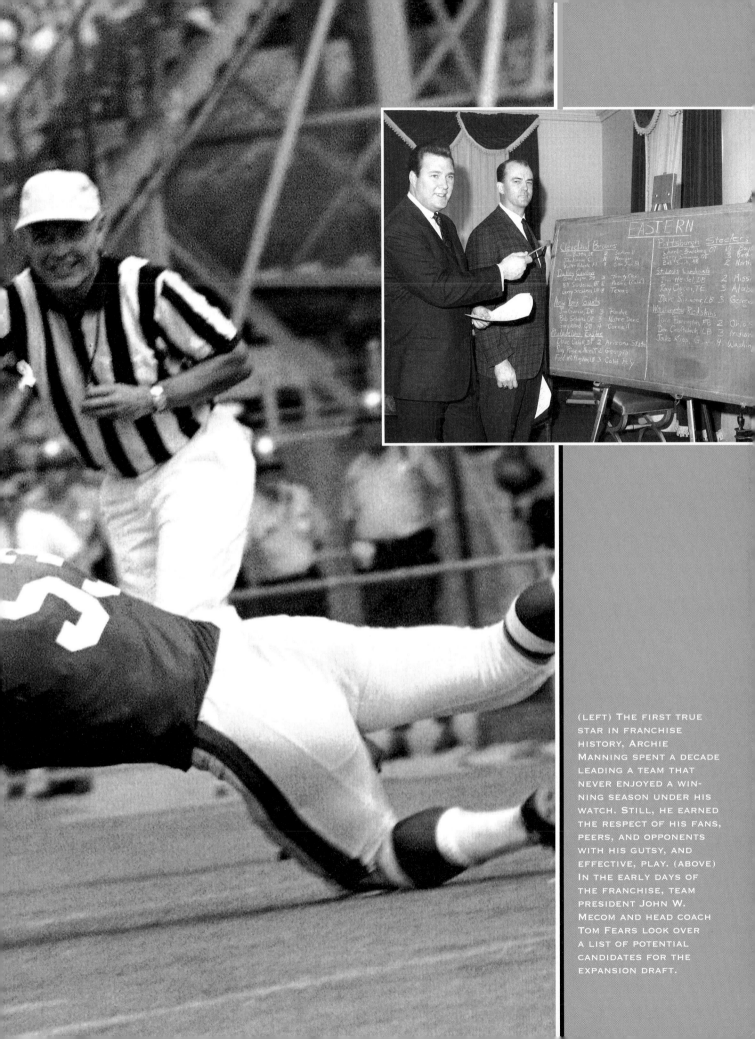

(LEFT) THE FIRST TRUE
STAR IN FRANCHISE
HISTORY, ARCHIE
MANNING SPENT A DECADE
LEADING A TEAM THAT
NEVER ENJOYED A WIN-
NING SEASON UNDER HIS
WATCH. STILL, HE EARNED
THE RESPECT OF HIS FANS,
PEERS, AND OPPONENTS
WITH HIS GUTSY, AND
EFFECTIVE, PLAY. (ABOVE)
IN THE EARLY DAYS OF
THE FRANCHISE, TEAM
PRESIDENT JOHN W.
MECOM AND HEAD COACH
TOM FEARS LOOK OVER
A LIST OF POTENTIAL
CANDIDATES FOR THE
EXPANSION DRAFT.

to change in 1986. That was when New Orleans automobile and banking tycoon Tom Benson bought the team and immediately cleaned house in the front office.

Benson hired general manager Jim Finks, who had built both the Minnesota Vikings and Chicago Bears into Super Bowl teams. Finks in turn hired head coach Jim Mora, who had won two championships in three years with the USFL's Philadelphia/Baltimore franchise.

The Saints went 6–10 in the first year under Finks and Mora, but finally broke through in 1987, going 12–3 and capturing an NFC wild-card berth. The jubilation was short-lived, however, as New Orleans lost 44–10 to Minnesota in its playoff debut.

Buoyed by such star players as Rickey Jackson, Sam Mills, Bobby Hebert, and Dalton Hilliard, the Saints would return to the playoffs in 1990, 1991, and 1992, but still failed to win a postseason game. The team got progressively worse throughout the mid-1990s, and Mora eventually resigned, replaced by longtime Bears coach Mike Ditka, whose teams performed no better.

It was under Jim Haslett that the Saints finally tasted playoff glory in 2000, beating St. Louis 31–28 in the wild-card round before falling to Minnesota 34–16 the following week. Like Mora and Ditka before him, however, Haslett's teams got progressively worse and he was fired after the 2005 season.

That 2005 season deserves special mention, however, given the conditions under which it was played. Hurricane Katrina struck the Gulf Coast two weeks before the season opener, leaving the Superdome, and most of the city of New Orleans, uninhabitable. The Saints split their home games between Baton Rouge and San Antonio, and limped home with a 3–13 record.

Fortunes finally began to turn in 2006, when New Orleans had a new coach (Sean Payton), quarterback (Drew Brees), and franchise player (Reggie Bush). The Saints beat Atlanta 23–3 in spectacular fashion in their return to the Dome on September 25, and rode that momentum all the way to the NFC Championship Game, where they lost to the Chicago Bears 39–14.

The Saints sank back into mediocrity in 2007 and 2008, going a combined 15–17 despite record-setting performances by Brees and the team's offense. But everything finally fell into place in 2009, for New Orleans and its beloved Saints. ❧

TOM DEMPSEY'S RECORD 63-YARD FIELD GOAL WAS ONE OF THE FEW HIGHLIGHTS IN THE EARLY DECADES FOR THE SAINTS. HIS BOOT HAS BEEN EQUALED BY JASON ELAM BUT NEVER SURPASSED.

OFF AND ROLLING

SAINTS 45, LIONS 27 • SEPTEMBER 13, 2009 • LOUISIANA SUPERDOME, NEW ORLEANS

After finishing the preseason with a 3–1 record, the Saints were heavy favorites heading into their 2009 season opener. Not only was New Orleans playing at a sold-out and festive Louisiana Superdome, but they were facing the Detroit Lions, the NFL's doormat in 2008 with a 0–16 record. The Lions were also set to start No. 1 overall pick Matthew Stafford, a rookie quarterback making his NFL debut on the road.

Nevertheless, the Saints had a few personnel issues to sort out before the game. Starting left tackle Jammal Brown, a two-time Pro Bowl selection, was set to miss the game with a sports hernia (he would eventually sit out the entire season following surgery), leaving third-year pro Jermon Bushrod to start in Brown's place at a key offensive-line position.

Also, the club elected to start defensive ends Charles Grant and Will Smith, who had been suspended four games each for violating league policy late in the 2008 season, but had appealed the penalty (they would eventually be cleared play the entire season). Perhaps most significantly, starting running back Pierre Thomas was out with a knee injury, meaning free-agent signee Mike Bell was set to get the bulk of the carries in the running game.

Despite all that, anticipation for the season-opener was at an all-time high. "We're all excited," quarterback

Drew Brees said. "It's been a good and tough camp, very competitive, but that's what you pay the price for to have the chance to go out there on Sundays during the regular season and play for keeps and play when it counts. This is what we're waiting for."

It was Brees whose star shone brightest on this day, as the All-Pro quarterback passed for a career-high six touchdown passes and 358 yards in a 45–27 rout of the Lions. Brees' touchdown total tied a Saints record that went all the way back to 1969, when Billy Kilmer also threw for six TDs against the St. Louis Cardinals.

Brees threw four touchdown passes in the first half, including on each of the Saints' first two possessions as New Orleans led 14–0 less than six minutes into the game. He hit Marques Colston for 9 yards and Robert Meachem for 39, giving the Saints a 14–3 lead after one quarter.

Detroit cut the lead to 14–10 on Kevin Smith's 4-yard run early in the second quarter, but New Orleans came right back with two more scores before halftime to lead 28–10 at the break. Brees threw touchdown passes of 1 and 15 yards to tight end Jeremy Shockey–who failed to catch a touchdown during an injury-plagued 2008 season–his first with the Saints after a highly publicized trade from the New York Giants.

"It was satisfying," Shockey said. "I'm…happy to get the win and what better place to do it than the

JEREMY SHOCKEY CELEBRATES THE FIRST OF HIS TWO SECOND-QUARTER TOUCHDOWNS, HELPING TO PUT SAINTS AHEAD 28–10 AT HALFTIME. SHOCKEY'S TIMELY GRABS TURNED A 14–10 GAME INTO A ROUT, AS THE SAINTS NEVER LED BY FEWER THAN 11 THE REST OF THE WAY.

dome. The fans were great today. They definitely helped us out. Hopefully, we will get a lot more wins this year and have a lot of fun doing it."

A wild third quarter saw the Saints outscored 17–10 by the Lions, who generated points on Stafford's 1-yard run, Jason Hanson's 24-yard field goal, and Louis Delmas' 65-yard return of Bell's fumble. New Orleans scored on John Carney's 38-yard field goal and a 58-yard Brees–to–Devery-Henderson touchdown pass to lead 38–27 after three.

Brees hit fullback Heath Evans for a 13-yard touchdown in the fourth quarter to close out the scoring. The Saints outgained the Lions 515 yards to 231, but still made enough mistakes—three turnovers, allowing a long kickoff return, having a field goal blocked—to keep head coach Sean Payton from being too happy following the game. "There were enough sloppy things that really force us to look closely at cleaning those things up," Payton said. "That is really what I told (the team). I was excited for the win, and yet there are a number of things that we have to do better and handle better."

Despite his fumble, Bell enjoyed a fine debut for New Orleans, rushing for 143 yards on 28 carries. Henderson led all receivers with 103 yards on five catches.

New Orleans' retooled defense made life rough for Stafford, who went 16 for 37 for 205 yards and three interceptions in his debut. Saints free safety Darren Sharper, another offseason acquisition, intercepted two of those passes, while linebacker Scott Shanle had the other as New Orleans won its season-opener for the fourth time in five years. ❧

NEW ORLEANS SAINTS VS. DETROIT LIONS

	1	2	3	4	FINAL	
Detroit	3	7	17	0	27	Record: (0-1)
New Orleans	14	14	10	7	45	Record: (1-0)

MIKE BELL TURNS THE CORNER AS THE LIONS DEFENSE FLAILS AWAY. HE CARRIED 28 TIMES FOR 143 YARDS AGAINST DETROIT, BOTH SEASON HIGHS FOR A BACK THAT WAS ON HIS WAY TO HIS BEST SEASON SINCE 2006 WITH DENVER.

OFFENSIVE FIREWORKS CONTINUE

SAINTS 48, EAGLES 22 • SEPTEMBER 20, 2009 • LINCOLN FINANCIAL FIELD, PHILADELPHIA, PENNSYLVANIA

Leaving the Louisiana Superdome did little to slow down the New Orleans Saints' juggernaut offense in its road opener at Philadelphia in Week 2. The Saints once again piled up the points and big plays, scoring a 48–22 victory at Lincoln Financial Field. Quarterback Drew Brees threw only half as many touchdown passes as he did in the season-opening win over Detroit but still managed 311 yards and three touchdowns to help New Orleans improve to 2–0 on the year.

Brees completed 25 of 34 passes, with nine different receivers catching at least one pass. Only Marques Colston (8 receptions, 98 yards, 2 TDs) managed more than four receptions all day. "If you look at our skill group, each game no guy ever knows who's day it's gonna be," Brees said. "Each guy knows it's their job to open things up for everyone else."

Injuries continued to be an issue for the Saints, who lost receiver Lance Moore early in the game with a pulled hamstring and got only one series of out starting tailback Pierre Thomas, who had missed the season-opener with a sprained knee. But the big injury news of the day involved Eagles quarterback Donovan McNabb, who sat out with a cracked rib.

That left Kevin Kolb to make his first NFL start at quarterback, and the third-year man from Houston certainly got his arm loose. Kolb threw for 391 yards and two touchdowns on 31-for-51 passing, but also threw three interceptions. The last of those picks resulted in a 97-yard touchdown return by Darren Sharper, a runback that tied a Saints record for the longest in team history. Sharper continued his fast start in his first year with the club, having totaled three interceptions through two games in Black and Gold.

"This is a very good team we played today, and this is a really tough place to play," Saints coach Sean Payton said. "I think looking back on it, I would say that the turnover battle was probably the deciding factor in the game today."

Two turnovers early in the third quarter turned a 17–13 halftime lead for the Saints into a 31–13 advantage in a matter of moments. Philadelphia's Ellis Hobbs fumbled the opening kickoff of the half, and New Orleans' Chris Reis recovered at the 22.

Brees hit fullback Heath Evans for an 11-yard score to make it 24–13, then Scott Shanle intercepted Kolb on the Eagles' next possession. Mike Bell's 7-yard touchdown run made it an 18-point lead with

DREW BREES PICKED UP RIGHT WHERE HE LEFT OFF AFTER TOSSING SIX TOUCHDOWN PASSES AGAINST DETROIT. HE TORCHED THE PHILADELPHIA SECONDARY FOR 311 YARDS AND THREW THREE MORE SCORES.

11:39 left in the third quarter.

John Carney's 25-yard field goal made it 34–13 before the Eagles cut the lead to 14 on Kolb's 3-yard pass to Jason Avant. The Saints dominated the fourth quarter, getting Reggie Bush's 19-yard touchdown run and Sharper's long interception to just a safety for Philadelphia.

The first half was more closely contested, as the teams exchanged touchdowns in the early going. Brees connected with Colston on a 15-yard strike to put New Orleans up 7–0, then Philadelphia answered with Kolb's 71-yard scoring pass to DeSean Jackson. Carney and David Akers swapped field goals to make it 10–10 early in the second quarter, then Brees and Colston hooked up again–this time from 25 yards out–to put the Saints up 17–10. Akers' 32-yard field goal made it a four-point game at halftime.

Bell rushed for 86 yards and a touchdown on 17 carries before leaving the game with his own sprained knee. Bush filled in admirably, totaling 75 yards on 13 touches rushing and receiving. Devery Henderson managed 71 yards on three receptions, while Jeremy Shockey caught four passes for 49 yards.

Shanle had a solid all-around game on defense with 11 tackles and the interception, while second-year man Tracy Porter notched his first pickoff of the year. The 2-0 start was the Saints' first since 2006, Payton's first season with the club. "You like starting 2-0, but it doesn't promise you anything," Payton said. ∞

NEW ORLEANS SAINTS AT PHILADELPHIA EAGLES

	1	2	3	4	FINAL	
New Orleans	10	7	17	14	48	Record: (2–0)
Philadelphia	7	6	7	2	22	Record: (1–1)

BOBBY MCCRAY PLANTS HIS HEAD FIRMLY BETWEEN KEVIN KOLB'S SHOULDERS AS HE DRIVES INTO THE PHILADELPHIA QUARTERBACK. KOLB THREW FOR 391 YARDS IN HIS FIRST NFL START BUT WAS INTERCEPTED THREE TIMES, ONCE FOR A TOUCHDOWN.

NEW ORLEANS SHUTS DOWN T.O., BUFFALO

SAINTS 27, BILLS 7 • SEPTEMBER 27, 2009 • RALPH WILSON STADIUM, BUFFALO, NEW YORK

Two weeks into the 2009 season, the New Orleans Saints had firmly established themselves as an offensive juggernaut, capable of scoring big on any team. Still, the team's defense remained suspect. The Saints had forced a number of turnovers in wins over Detroit and Philadelphia but had also surrendered an uncomfortable amount of yards and points to each.

That changed, at least temporarily, in Week 3 against the Buffalo Bills. The Saints' defense posted one of its better efforts of the season, allowing just a touchdown and holding All-Pro receiver Terrell Owens without a catch in a 27–7 victory on a blustery day in Buffalo.

"It was a total team effort," cornerback Jabari Greer said. "We just wanted to come back because we knew how these guys play. We didn't fall back or let up. We showed great resilience. The defensive line got on the quarterback and the linebackers secured tackles. It was great to get a win. But it was better given the way the defense and offense played."

The Saints' defense totaled four sacks and two turnovers, more than making up for a less-than-stellar effort by New Orleans' high-powered passing game. Quarterback Drew Brees did not throw a touchdown

pass and finished with just 172 yards through the air, his first sub-200-yard day in a span of 22 games.

Running back Pierre Thomas also picked up the slack in his first extended action of the season after sitting out most of the first two games with a knee injury. With leading rusher Mike Bell sidelined by his own knee problems, Thomas rushed for 126 yards and two fourth-quarter touchdowns on 14 carries despite battling flu-like symptoms all day.

"I can't say enough about him and what he fought through today, being sick, battling through injuries, he is a warrior," Brees said. "The offensive line did a tremendous job opening up those holes. His fullback Heath Evans did a tremendous job."

After one drive, however, it looked like another offensive explosion by the Saints, who drove 81 yards in 10 plays with the opening kickoff. Brees converted two third downs with passes to Marques Colston, and short-yardage back Lynell Hamilton punched the ball into the end zone for a 1-yard score and a 7–0 New Orleans lead with 10:04 to play in the first.

That would be the only offensive touchdown for either team in the first half, though Buffalo used special teams to get into the end zone early in the second

PIERRE THOMAS SEARCHES FOR SOME OF HIS 126 RUSHING YARDS. HIS ENTIRE TOTAL CAME DURING THE SECOND HALF, AND HIS TWO FOURTH-QUARTER TOUCHDOWNS SEALED THE WIN.

quarter. Holder Brad Moorman perfectly executed a fake field goal, hitting end Ryan Denney in stride for a 25-yard touchdown to make it 7–7 just 12 seconds into the quarter.

New Orleans took the lead back at 10–7 on John Carney's 27-yard field goal following a forced fumble by Malcolm Jenkins midway through the second quarter, but neither team would score again until the fourth quarter. The Saints' defense made a key stand late in the third quarter, as Greer tipped a ball intended for Owens into the hands of defensive end Will Smith, stopping a Buffalo drive cold at the New Orleans 27.

The Saints scored on three straight possessions in the fourth quarter to finally put the game away. Thomas raced into the end zone from 34 yards out to make it 17–7, then Carney connected on a 35-yard field goal to put New Orleans up 20–7 with 3:21 to play.

New Orleans then stopped Buffalo on downs, setting up Thomas' 19-yard touchdown run and a 20-point lead with 2:03 remaining. But the capper was shutting out Owens, who had caught a pass in 185 straight games dating back to his rookie season of 1996, the third-longest streak in NFL history behind Jerry Rice (274) and Marvin Harrison (190).

"It's always a victory for us when we can take away one of their top receivers," cornerback Tracy Porter said. "We didn't let him get any catches and that had a lot to do with getting pressure on the QB (Trent Edwards). They were forced to check down a lot. That was a victory for us." ◌

NEW ORLEANS SAINTS AT BUFFALO BILLS

	1	2	3	4	FINAL	
New Orleans	7	3	0	17	27	Record: (3–0)
Buffalo	0	7	0	0	7	Record: (1–2)

UPENDED BUT STILL HOLDING ON TO THE BALL, JEREMY SHOCKEY COMES DOWN WITH ONE OF HIS SIX RECEPTIONS. AFTER THROWING FOR NINE TOUCHDOWNS IN THE FIRST TWO GAMES OF THE SEASON, DREW BREES WAS HELD WITHOUT A TOUCHDOWN PASS DESPITE THROWING FOR 172 YARDS.

SHARPER THAN EVER

SAINTS 24, N.Y. JETS 10 • OCTOBER 4, 2009 • LOUISIANA SUPERDOME, NEW ORLEANS

Week 4's game between the New Orleans Saints and New York Jets promised to be one of the more intriguing match-ups of the early part of the 2009 NFL season, the unstoppable offense against the impenetrable defense. It also pitted a pair of quarterbacks who had led their teams to unbeaten starts, established star Drew Brees for the Saints and brash newcomer Mark Sanchez for the Jets.

By game's end, Brees had one-upped his young counterpart—at least on the scoreboard—leading New Orleans to a 24–10 victory at the Superdome. But credit a major assist once again to the Saints' defense, especially Darren Sharper.

The veteran safety, who joined New Orleans in the offseason as a free agent, intercepted two Sanchez passes, one of which he returned 99 yards for a touchdown in the second quarter. The Saints scored two defensive touchdowns in all, running their record to 4–0 for the first time since 1993.

Sharper's touchdown was his second of the season and 10th of his career, moving him into second place all-time behind only Hall-of-Famer Rod Woodson, who had 12 interception returns for scores during his days with the Pittsburgh Steelers, San Francisco 49ers, Oakland Raiders, and Baltimore Ravens. Sharper's 99-yard interception return gave New Orleans a 10–0 lead and forever turned the game's momentum in favor of the Saints, who struggled to put points on the board offensively against the Jets' attacking scheme.

"I think Sharp's been a great addition," Brees said. "Obviously you look at his productivity over the first four games—five interceptions, two returned for touchdowns. That's pretty impressive."

For the fourth straight game, New Orleans scored on its first offensive possession, getting John Carney's 34-yard field goal to make it 3–0 with 8:06 left in the opening quarter. But that was all the Saints' offense could muster in the first half, and that three-point lead held up until the first play of the second quarter.

Sanchez had driven the Jets all the way to the New Orleans 15, where he faced second-and-8. He looked for tight end Dustin Keller near the goal line on the left side, but Sharper jumped the route and sailed untouched 99 yards to the end zone for a 10–0 Saints lead.

"What this defense allows him to do with (defensive coordinator) Gregg Williams' style and aggressiveness and pressure, it really allows Sharper to do what he does best—and that's sit back and be the quarterback of the defense," Brees said. "He's a veteran player, he's been around, he's seen a lot, and he's played at a high level for a long time. He can read route combinations and jump certain routes. He can just play ball and play his type of football. He's been able to come up with some big plays."

REGGIE BUSH HURDLES OVER THE JETS DEFENSE. THE 4–0 START WAS THE FIRST FOR THE FRANCHISE SINCE THE 1993 TEAM STARTED THE YEAR 5–0.

The Saints drove all the way to the Jets' 1-yard line on their next possession, but two runs (one each by Pierre Thomas and Heath Evans) and two incomplete passes by Brees turned the ball over on downs. The Jets took over from there, but gave the Saints a touchdown on their second play when end Will Smith sacked Sanchez in the end zone, forcing a fumble that tackle Remi Ayodele fell on for a score and a 17–0 New Orleans lead.

The Jets got back in the game with back-to-back scores–Jay Feely's 38-yard field goal just before half-time and Thomas Jones' 15-yard touchdown run in the third quarter–to pull within 17–10, but the Saints controlled the fourth quarter. Thomas capped an 11-play, 74-yard drive with a 1-yard touchdown run to give New Orleans a 14-point lead with 6:07 to play.

The Saints ended any chance of a New York comeback by intercepting Sanchez on the Jets' next two possessions, once by Sharper and once by Randall Gay. The rookie quarterback finished a forgettable day 14 for 27 for 138 yards with three interceptions, plus the fumble.

"My mistakes killed us. They absolutely killed us," Sanchez said. "The defense played well enough to win. That whole game is 10–10 without three interceptions and a fumble. You turn the ball over like that in this league, and you can't win."

Brees, named the NFL's Offensive Player of the Month for September prior to the game, finished 20 for 32 for 190 yards, his second straight sub-200 yard day. Thomas keyed a strong running game with 86 yards and a touchdown on 19 carries. ◌

NEW ORLEANS SAINTS VS. N.Y. JETS						
	1	2	3	4	FINAL	
N.Y. Jets	0	3	7	0	10	Record: (3–1)
New Orleans	3	14	0	7	24	Record: (4–0)

ROBERT MEACHEM BREAKS THROUGH AN ARM TACKLE IN THE JETS SECONDARY. DREW BREES WAS HELD WITHOUT A TOUCHDOWN PASS FOR THE SECOND STRAIGHT WEEK BUT THE NEW ORLEANS DEFENSE WAS STOUT, SCORING TWICE TO PROVIDE THE COMFORTABLE WIN.

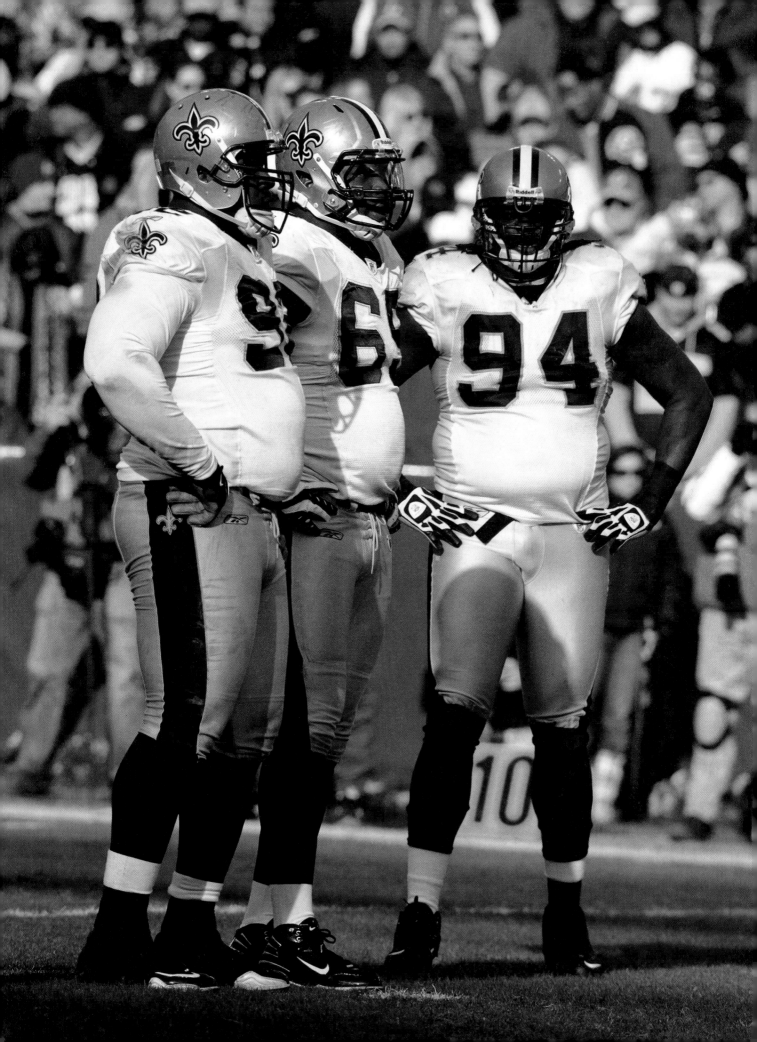

PIECING TOGETHER A PLAY-MAKING DEFENSE

I f ever a defense was more than the sum of its parts, it's the New Orleans Saints. New Orleans ranks in the lower-middle part of the NFL pack in most defensive categories—25th in total defense, 26th in pass defense, 21st in rush defense, etc., but near the top in one all-important category. Sean Payton's Saints forced 39 turnovers in 2009, ranking one behind league leader Green Bay, and scored eight defensive touchdowns.

"I think that's a huge part of our success so far, being able to turn over the ball, being able to score when we do get the turnovers and change the game," defensive end Will Smith said. "Coach Payton talks about how big the turnovers are through the course of the game. And if we can win the turnover battle, we have a high chance of winning, so that's huge."

The Saints' defensive transformation from league pushover to big-play unit has been a steady process, and began as soon as Payton arrived in 2006. But the New Orleans defense really began to take form in the last two seasons.

Of the Saints' 15 defensive regulars, 10 have joined the team since the start of the 2008 season and only two (starting ends Smith and Charles Grant) were inherited from the previous coaching regime. Grant (who was placed on injured reserve at the end of the regular season) and Smith were first-round picks in 2002 and 2004, respectively.

Payton and his staff added three current starters upon their arrival in 2006, strong safety Roman Harper (second-round draft pick), strong side linebacker Scott Fujita (free agency) and weak side linebacker Scott Shanle (trade). Fujita and Shanle had both played the 2005 season in Dallas, where Payton was quarterbacks coach and assistant head coach.

Six current standouts joined the club in 2008, including two in the draft's first two rounds: tackle Sedrick Ellis and cornerback Tracy Porter. Defensive end Bobby McCray and nickel back Randall Gay each came aboard as free agents, while nose tackle Remi Ayodele was signed off waivers from Dallas.

But the key transaction that offseason was a trade for middle linebacker Jonathan Vilma, coming off an injury-shortened year with the New York Jets. But Payton and general manager Mickey Loomis saw past Vilma's knee injury to a player who had totaled more than 100 tackles in each of his three healthy seasons and possessed uncanny leadership skills.

"I think most importantly does the player fit? Do you have a vision for the player?," Payton said. "I think in Jon's case we did, and it fit the scheme. We met him

AFTER A MIDDLING 2009 SEASON, NEW COORDINATOR GREGG WILLIAMS REVAMPED THE OUTLOOK FOR THE 2009 DEFENSIVE UNIT. IT ALL STARTS UP FRONT WITH THE DEFENSIVE LINE, EXPECTED TO GET THE INITIAL PENETRATION TO PUT PRESSURE ON OPPOSING OFFENSES.

at the (NFL Scouting) Combine, had a chance to visit with him there, and we were able to on eventually work the trade with New York."

Vilma had an outstanding 2008 season for the Saints, but the team continued to struggle defensively, ranking near the bottom of the league in all major categories. The overhaul continued in the offseason, as New Orleans spent its first-round draft pick on a cornerback (Malcolm Jenkins), brought another on board as a free agent (Jabari Greer) and also signed pass-rushing specialist Anthony Hargrove.

The two biggest acquisitions came prior to the draft, however. Longtime NFL defensive guru Gregg Williams signed on as the Saints' coordinator in mid-January, bringing with him a track record of fielding standout units at stops in Tennessee, Buffalo, Jacksonville, and Washington.

Williams installed an attacking-style scheme, one that began paying immediate dividends. The Saints forced four turnovers in their season-opener against Detroit and have hardly slowed since.

"I wouldn't say the attitude has changed where now all of a sudden we're just bigger, meaner, tougher guys," Payton said. "That is not the attitude that's changed. I think the way we go about practice, the way we focus on the details, I think that's changed."

The man who would prove to be Williams' coach on the field joined the team in March. Free safety Darren Sharper, one of the top defensive playmakers of the last decade, signed as a free agent after being cast off as too old by the Minnesota Vikings.

Sharper proved himself anything but on-the-decline with an All-Pro season in New Orleans. He intercepted nine passes, three of which he returned for touchdowns, two from 90-plus yards out.

"I think the main thing when people talk about changing the culture of our defense was just becoming a playmaking defense—something I've done in the past, something I kind of brought here," Sharper said. "Our turnover numbers have increased. I think that is something I've carried with me throughout my career with whatever defense I've been a part of." ∞

SAFETY ROMAN HARPER, WHO HAD 102 TACKLES IN THE REGULAR SEASON, TAKES DOWN BRETT FAVRE IN THE NFC CHAMPIONSHIP GAME.

A "GIANT" STEP

SAINTS 48, N.Y. GIANTS 27 • OCTOBER 18, 2009 • LOUISIANA SUPERDOME, NEW ORLEANS

Any lingering doubts as to whether or not the 2009 New Orleans Saints were for real as championship contenders were quickly and decisively put to rest in Week 6 of the regular season. The Saints stormed out of their bye week with one of their most dominant performances of the season on October 18, throttling the New York Giants 48--27 in a match-up of unbeaten teams. Drew Brees ended a personal two-game mini-slump with a four-touchdown afternoon, torching New York for 369 yards through the air as part of a 493-yard outburst that saw seven different players score touchdowns for 5–0 New Orleans.

Running back Pierre Thomas, who rushed for a team-best 72 yards in the game, said he believed the Saints made a "statement" with their victory. "Definitely, we knew we were going against a great team with a tough defense," Thomas said. "They have a good offense with a great quarterback. We had to come out here and really take it to them. We knew we were going to have our hands full. I believe we did a heck of a job."

As it had done in every game to that point in the season, New Orleans scored on its opening possession. A 15-play, 70-yard drive took 7:41 off the clock, ending in Mike Bell's 2-yard touchdown run on fourth-and-1, giving the Saints a 7–0 lead with 7:19 left in the first quarter.

After forcing the Giants to punt, New Orleans got the ball in the end zone again, this time on Brees' 1-yard touchdown pass to Jeremy Shockey. The tight end's touchdown came against his former team, for which he won a Super Bowl ring following the 2007 season.

"It's something special anytime you can get a win in this league," Shockey said. "It makes it special beating a team that was 5–0. I'd be lying if I said it didn't feel a little bit better than some teams. I had been in that system for six years and know a lot of the players, coaches, and trainers. It was a little awkward, but it was all about getting that win."

The Giants picked up Lawrence Tynes' 50-yard field goal to make it 14–3 at the end of the first quarter, but would never seriously threaten, as New Orleans answered with another touchdown. Brees' 36-yard scoring pass to Robert Meachem made it 20–3 with 12:40 to play before halftime (Carney's extra point was blocked).

The remainder of the first half saw both teams score twice, New Orleans on a 12-yard scoring pass from Brees to Lance Moore and a 7-yard run by Reggie Bush, and New York on Ahmad Bradshaw's 10-yard run and Eli Manning's 15-yard touchdown pass to Mario Manningham. Despite the offensive surge by the Giants, the Saints still led 34–17 at the half.

New Orleans extended its lead to 41–17 in the

JEREMY SHOCKEY CATCHES A TOUCHDOWN PASS IN THE FIRST HALF AGAINST HIS FORMER TEAM.

third quarter on Brees' final touchdown pass of the night, a 12-yarder to Marques Colston. Tynes kicked a 38-yarder to make it 41–20 early in the fourth quarter, but fullback Heath Evans ran in from 2 yards out to put the Saints on top by 28. The Giants had pulled their starters by that point, with back-up quarterback David Carr hitting rookie Hakeem Nicks for a 37-yard touchdown pass to complete the scoring with 3:15 to play.

Brees was once again dead-on accurate for the Saints, finishing 23-for-30 passing. Colston led all receivers with eight catches for 166 yards, while Moore enjoyed his best game of an injury-plagued season with six receptions for 78 yards.

After such a decisive win, the only challenge remaining for the Saints was to remain grounded as the words "Super Bowl" were seriously being discussed among the fanbase and the media.

"I don't really think that's an issue in this locker room," Colston said. "This group has been together long enough to see some of the great times and the last two years have been pretty difficult for us, so staying grounded is definitely not an issue in this locker room. We have some great veteran leadership and guys just know how to handle their business." ○

NEW ORLEANS SAINTS VS. N.Y. GIANTS						
	1	2	3	4	FINAL	
N.Y. Giants	3	14	0	10	27	Record: (5–1)
New Orleans	14	20	7	7	48	Record: (5–0)

THE SAINTS DEFENSE SWARMS TO DROP NEW YORK'S DOMENIK HIXON. GIANTS QUARTERBACK ELI MANNING HAD A RUDE HOMECOMING IN HIS FIRST GAME AT THE SUPERDOME, HAVING TO WORK FOR EACH OF HIS 14 COMPLETIONS AND LOOKING HAGGARD BEFORE BEING REPLACED BY DAVID CARR.

A COMEBACK FOR THE AGES

SAINTS 46, DOLPHINS 34 • OCTOBER 25, 2009 • LANDSHARK STADIUM, MIAMI GARDENS, FLORIDA

It was the kind of deficit many New Orleans Saints teams had faced in the past, and the vast majority of them had resigned themselves to defeat. But once again, the 2009 Saints proved they were different. The Saints overcame a 21-point hole late in the first half to stay unbeaten, beating homestanding Miami 46–34 on the strength of a 34-point second half. It was New Orleans' biggest comeback win since 1987 and its fourth game in six that it had scored at least 45 points.

"There was no doubt on our sideline we would come back and win," quarterback Drew Brees said. "They had given us their best shot, and we had played about as bad as we could play. All we had to do was string together a few drives and gain the momentum back. We knew it was going to happen, and it did."

The final stat line showed Brees posted one of his worst days as a Saint, throwing three interceptions, losing a fumble, and enduring five sacks. But he also led three consecutive scoring drives in the second half as New Orleans overcame a Miami team that led by as much as 24–3 early on.

The Saints defense also did its part once again, forcing three Miami turnovers and scoring twice. Darren Sharper recorded his third interception return for a touchdown of the season early in the third quarter, and Tracy Porter's 54-yard runback sealed the game in the final two minutes.

"It can be a season-defining win," linebacker Scott Shanle said. "This was a test we hadn't faced yet, and we couldn't be happier with the way we responded."

Despite the absence of starting quarterback Chad Pennington (out for the season after shoulder surgery), Miami looked for much of the first half like it was going to run away with the game. Former Saint Ricky Williams rushed for two touchdowns (4 yards and 68 yards), Ronnie Brown rushed for a third (8 yards), and Dan Carpenter added a 32-yard field goal. All New Orleans could manage was a 46-yard John Carney field goal to trail 24–3 late in the first half.

It was with five seconds left in the half that Brees exerted his now-legendary leadership skills after an apparent touchdown pass to Marques Colston was overturned by replay review. During the timeout, Brees talked Saints coach Sean Payton into going for the touchdown rather than kicking a field goal, and Brees snuck the ball into the end zone to cut the Miami lead to 14 points at halftime.

"I just told him I'd get it," Brees said. "I said, 'I'll

DESPITE HAVING SOME TROUBLE EARLY IN THE GAME, THE SAINTS OFFENSE WARMED UP LATE. BY THE TIME THE DUST HAD SETTLED, THEY HAD SCORED 40 POINTS FOR THE FOURTH TIME IN SIX GAMES.

get the touchdown. I know exactly what to do.'"

The New Orleans rally continued with Sharper's 42-yard pick-6 and a 10-yard Brees-to-Colston touchdown pass in the third quarter. Nevertheless, Miami stayed up by 10 on the strength of a Carpenter field goal and Williams' third touchdown of the day, a 4-yarder that gave the Dolphins a 34–24 advantage after three quarters.

The fourth quarter belonged to the Saints, however, as New Orleans scored the first three times it had the ball. Brees hit Jeremy Shockey for 66 yards on the final play of the third quarter, setting up Reggie Bush's 10-yard touchdown run to pull the Saints within 34–31.

After Miami went three-and-out, Brees hit Shockey twice for first downs and then ran in from two yards out to put New Orleans on top for the first time at 37–34 (Carney's extra point attempt was wide left). Carney hit a 20-yarder to make it 40–34 with 3:21 to play. Porter's touchdown moments later finished off the wild comeback.

"There were a lot of things that we didn't do well in the first half," Saints coach Sean Payton said. "But that's because Miami did a lot of things and played very well in the first half. We talked at halftime about playing four quarters.… It was the first chance for us to play from a deficit, and I was encouraged with how we responded."

Brees totaled just one scoring pass in the game, but did record the first two-touchdown rushing day of his career. Shockey led all receivers with 105 yards on four catches, while Carney became the fourth player in NFL history to surpass the 2,000-point mark in career scoring.

One sour note for the Saints involved starting fullback and standout blocker Heath Evans, who was lost for the season after a fourth-quarter knee injury. ◌

NEW ORLEANS SAINTS AT MIAMI DOLPHINS

	1	2	3	4	FINAL	
New Orleans	3	7	14	22	46	Record: (6–0)
Miami	14	10	10	0	34	Record: (2–4)

REGGIE BUSH LEAPS AND REACHES FOR THE PYLON ON HIS 10-YARD TOUCHDOWN RUN IN THE FOURTH QUARTER. THE SCORE HELPED BRING THE SAINTS WITHIN THREE. THEY SCORED THE NEXT 15 POINTS TO COMPLETE THE COMEBACK AND PUT THE DOLPHINS AWAY.

NO MONDAY NIGHT MASTERPIECE

SAINTS 35, FALCONS 27 • NOVEMBER 2, 2009 • LOUISIANA SUPERDOME, NEW ORLEANS

*M*onday Night Football did not bring out the best in the New Orleans Saints like it did the last time the team met the Atlanta Falcons on a national stage. But a sloppy Saints effort was still enough to match the best start in franchise history. The Saints turned the ball over four times for the second straight week and for the second straight week recorded a comeback victory. Three unanswered touchdowns in the second quarter made the difference, as New Orleans beat Atlanta 35–27 and ran its record to 7–0 for the first time since 1991.

The victory was not as decisive as New Orleans' 23–3 victory over Atlanta in 2006, a Monday night game that marked the team's return to the Louisiana Superdome for the first time since Hurricane Katrina. But it was a key victory against a fellow NFC South Division contender, with the loss dropping the Falcons three games behind the Saints in the standings.

"I'm excited to win this game and get to 7–0," Saints coach Sean Payton said. "It was an important game against a division team. It wasn't perfect; it wasn't clean."

Each team used the ground game to score on their opening possession, Atlanta getting a 13-yard touchdown run by Michael Turner to lead 7–0 and New

Orleans answering with a 22-yard scamper by Pierre Thomas to tie it. The Saints' first big mistake gave Atlanta a 14–7 lead after one quarter, as Thomas DeCoud sacked Brees into a fumble and Kroy Biermann picked up the loose ball and rambled for a 4-yard touchdown.

New Orleans owned the second quarter, however, getting Brees' 18-yard TD pass to Marques Colston and Reggie Bush's 1-yard run to lead 21–7 with 42 seconds left in the half. The Saints' big-play defense tacked on a score just before the half—its sixth touchdown of the year—on Jabari Greer's 48-yard interception return.

"They had ran that route a few times to my side," said Greer, acquired via free agency from the Buffalo Bills in the offseason. "I broke it up the first time they threw that play, but I knew that wasn't going to be good enough against this offense. Fortunately, I was lucky enough to get another opportunity. I was able to go out there and catch a ball. The defensive guys created a lane with their blocks. I got down the numbers and took it in."

Atlanta scored the game's next 10 points, on a 68-yard scoring strike from Matt Ryan to Roddy White and a 25-yard field goal from Jason Elam, to pull within

TIGHT END DAVID THOMAS HELPS MARQUES COLSTON CELEBRATE HIS 18-YARD TOUCHDOWN RECEPTION IN THE SECOND QUARTER. THE SAINTS TURNED THE BALL OVER FOUR TIMES BUT THE TEAM WAS PLAYING SO WELL THAT THEY COULD NOT EVEN BEAT THEMSELVES.

28–24 with 11:33 left in the game. The Saints did themselves no favors in the meantime, with John Carney missing a short field goal and Thomas fumbling the ball away at the New Orleans 34 with 10 minutes remaining.

That was when the Saints' defense again stood tall, with middle linebacker Jonathan Vilma tipping a Ryan pass into the hands of cornerback Tracy Porter at the New Orleans 1-yard line. Porter ran the ball back out to the Saints' 19, and the Atlanta threat was over.

"It was huge," free safety Darren Sharper said of Porter's interception. "That had to be the play of the game. They were driving to go up. We get that interception and didn't allow any points. That was big. We have done a good job of making big plays in the red zone. That has kind of been the staple of our defense. It's big preventing them from scoring."

New Orleans then moved 81 yards in 11 plays, a drive kept alive by a defensive holding call against Atlanta on third-and-5 from the Saints' 24. Brees later hit Colston for 29 yards, tight end Jeremy Shockey for 17 and Thomas for a 1-yard touchdown to make it 35–24 with 3:03 remaining in the game.

Atlanta battled back for Elam's 40-yard field goal to cut the Saints' lead to 8, then recovered an onside kick for one last chance to tie the game. But Ryan's final pass was intercepted by Sharper at the New Orleans 5-yard line with three seconds to play, and the Saints had their seventh straight victory to open the season.

Brees ended the night 25 for 33 for 308 yards and two scores passing, while Thomas rushed for 91 yards and one touchdown while also adding another receiving. ✃

NEW ORLEANS SAINTS VS. ATLANTA FALCONS						
	1	2	3	4	FINAL	
Atlanta	14	0	7	6	27	Record: (4–3)
New Orleans	7	21	0	7	35	Record: (7–0)

COLSTON ELEVATES TO COME DOWN WITH ONE OF HIS SIX CATCHES. A THREE-TOUCHDOWN SECOND QUARTER PUT THE SAINTS AHEAD TO STAY, PUNCTUATED BY JABARI GREER'S 48-YARD INTERCEPTION RETURN FOR A SCORE.

A THIRD STRAIGHT COMEBACK VICTORY

SAINTS 30, PANTHERS 20 • NOVEMBER 8, 2009 • LOUISIANA SUPERDOME, NEW ORLEANS

Improbable rallies were beginning to become routine for the New Orleans Saints as the midway point of the 2009 season approached. And the Saints' 30–20 victory over Carolina on November 9 might have been the most unlikely of all.

The Saints fell behind 14–0 in the first quarter, and didn't take their first lead of the game until John Carney's 40-yard field goal put them on top 23–20 with 4:36 remaining. Moments later, New Orleans' big-play defense struck again—this time on Anthony Hargrove's 1-yard return of a DeAngelo Williams fumble—to clinch the victory and keep the Saints unbeaten at the halfway mark of the schedule for the first time in franchise history.

"The more you win games like this, the more confidence you gain," quarterback Drew Brees said. "You just feel like you're going to come back and you're going to do it. On the flip side, every team that comes in and plays you knows it's going to be a 60-minute game."

Unlike in previous weeks, New Orleans found itself down by a touchdown moments into the game against Carolina, which entered the day riding a three-game winning streak. Williams, the NFL's leading touchdown scorer in 2008, burst off right guard for a 66-yard score and a 7–0 lead on the Panthers' second play of the night.

Brees later fumbled inside his own 10-yard line to set up another quick score by Williams, this one a 7-yard run to give Carolina a 14–0 advantage at the end of the first quarter. Williams would end the night with 149 yards rushing but would not score again as New Orleans began to mount its comeback.

Brees engineered a 15-play drive the ended in John Carney's 23-yard field goal to make it 14–3, but Carolina answered with a John Kasay's 32-yarder to push the lead back to 14. Carney hit a 25-yarder with four seconds left to cut the deficit to 17–6 at the half.

"They started off pretty well against us," Saints defensive end Will Smith said. "We came out and we were a little over-excited and forgot what to do."

New Orleans broke out the big-play passing game to finally get into the end zone twice in the third quarter. Brees hit Devery Henderson for 63 yards, setting up Pierre Thomas' 10-yard run, which made it a 17–13 game with 13:14 left in the third.

Carolina then ground out a 19-play drive, but could manage only Kasay's 25-yard field goal for a 20–13 lead. The Saints went to the air again, with Brees

PIERRE THOMAS HAD TO SCRATCH AND CLAW FOR EVERY ONE OF HIS TEAM-LEADING 50 YARDS. HIS THIRD-QUARTER TOUCHDOWN BROUGHT THE SAINTS WITHIN STRIKING DISTANCE, AND ROBERT MEACHEM'S 54-YARD TOUCHDOWN CATCH LATER IN THE QUARTER TIED THE GAME.

hooking up with Robert Meachem for a 54-yard score. All of a sudden, the game was tied at 20 after three.

"Devery's pass was a third-and-5, man-to-man," Brees said. "He does a good job of beating the defender. The safety takes a bad angle. It was a great individual effort on his part. Lance (Moore) being down, as big a part of the offense as he is, (Henderson and Meachem) knew they would be a bigger part of the offense today. Obviously, they can really help us win and they did."

Carolina stalled out at the New Orleans 46 on its ensuing possession, and New Orleans drove for the go-ahead score after taking over on its own 2. Brees—who passed for 330 yards on the day—hit Thomas for 17 yards, Reggie Bush for 10, and Meachem for 21, moving the team into position for Carney's 40-yard field goal after a deep pass to Marques Colston failed to connect.

The Panthers fumbled the ball away on their next two possessions, with Hargrove coming up with the loose ball both times. First it was Smith sacking Jake Delhomme at the Saints' 48 to stop one drive with 2:43 to play, then it was Hargrove stripping the ball from Williams himself and bounding into the end zone to put New Orleans up 10 with 2:17 remaining.

Carolina drove back down as far as the Saints' 2, but turned the ball over on downs with 17 seconds remaining. Brees took a knee, and New Orleans was perfect at the halfway mark.

"It was good to get that win to get to 8–0," Saints coach Sean Payton said. "I am encouraged with how we have been able to win a few of these games without playing our best football. I am proud of how our players hung in there and battled back and got back in the game." ∞

NEW ORLEANS SAINTS VS. CAROLINA PANTHERS

	1	2	3	4	FINAL	
Carolina	14	3	3	0	20	Record: (3–5)
New Orleans	0	6	14	10	30	Record: (8–0)

THE SAINTS DEFENSE SWARMS TO DROP CAROLINA'S TYRELL SUTTON. THE 3–5 PANTHERS HAD ONE OF THEIR BETTER OFFENSIVE DAYS OF THE SEASON— INCLUDING 149 YARDS FROM JONATHAN STEWART— BUT IT WAS STILL FAR FROM ENOUGH TO SECURE A WIN.

BUSH, ROBY PROVIDE PUSH TO 9-0

SAINTS 28, RAMS 23 • NOVEMBER 15, 2009 • EDWARD JONES DOME, ST. LOUIS, MISSOURI

One key to a successful season is the ability to win despite not playing particularly well at times. The New Orleans Saints were the living embodiment of that old football maxim in Week 10 against St. Louis.

Reggie Bush scored two touchdowns and Courtney Roby ran the second-half kickoff back 97 yards for a score, as the Saints overcame three turnovers and numerous lapses in execution to remain perfect at 9-0. Homestanding St. Louis—which had won just once coming in—never led, but had the ball in Saints territory with a chance to win in the final seconds.

"I was pleased we got the win," Saints coach Sean Payton said. "It was a closer finish than I would have liked. And the turnovers will come back to bite us. I think it goes without saying that your entire roster has to be ready to play. I was pleased with how they responded."

The Saints continued to struggle early on offense, going scoreless in the first quarter for the second straight week. New Orleans did begin a 13-play scoring drive late in the opening period, which Bush capped with a 3-yard touchdown run for a 7-0 lead with 14:14 left in the half. St. Louis came right back, however, getting a 29-yard pass from Marc Bulger to Donnie Avery

to tie the game with 9:23 to go before the break.

New Orleans began its ensuing possession with a reverse to Robert Meachem for 41 yards, and Drew Brees found Bush for a 15-yard touchdown pass to put the Saints up 14–7. St. Louis again answered, this time behind running back Steven Jackson, who carried the ball on the last seven of a 13-play drive, scoring from two yards out to make it 14-all at the half.

"Steven Jackson is a hell of a running back," linebacker Scott Fujita said. "It was clear they wanted to run on first and second downs and pass on thirds."

The tie score would last only as long as it took Roby to sprint the length of the field, as the fifth-year pro out of Indiana supplied his first career kickoff return for a touchdown to open the second half and give New Orleans a 21–14 lead. It was the Saints' first kickoff return for a score since Michael Lewis turned the trick in 2004.

This time St. Louis could answer with only a 32-yard Josh Brown field goal to make it 21-17 but thwarted a potential Saints touchdown drive by forcing a turnover in the red zone. Brees hit Marques Colston at the 1-yard line, but safety Oshi Atogwe jarred the ball loose and it rolled through the end zone for a touchback.

DREW BREES WINDS UP AND FIRES DOWNFIELD. HE THREW FOR 223 YARDS AND A PAIR OF SCORES, THE LAST A 27-YARDER TO ROBERT MEACHEM THAT PROVIDED THE EVENTUAL WINNING POINTS.

Undaunted, the Saints forced the Rams to punt the ball back and drove 77 yards for their final touchdown. Brees hit Meachem for a 27-yard score, putting the Saints on top 28–17 with 12:15 to play.

Other times that might have been enough, but a botched fake punt gave St. Louis new life midway through the final quarter. St. Louis drove 80 yards to the end zone, with Bulger connecting with Avery again on a 19-yard touchdown pass. But the Rams could not convert on a two-point try and the Saints still led by 5 with 2:44 remaining.

Colston recovered an onside kick attempt for New Orleans, but the Saints could not hold onto the ball; Thomas Morstead punted the ball into the end zone for a touchback. St. Louis had one last chance to win but could get no closer than the Saints' 32-yard line before Bulger's last-second pass fell incomplete, and New Orleans could finally breathe easy.

"A win is a win in this league," cornerback Randall Gay said. "It's tough to win any game, much less one on the road. It's never easy. The records get thrown out when you line up. We just passed the halfway point of the season and there is still a lot of football to be played."

The Saints were beginning to accumulate injuries at an alarming rate, however. With Jabari Greer already out with a sports hernia that would sideline him until the regular-season finale, fellow corner Tracy Porter went down against St. Louis with a sprained knee ligament that would keep him out four weeks. Safety Darren Sharper (knee) missed the St. Louis game but would return the following week against Tampa Bay. ◌

NEW ORLEANS SAINTS AT ST. LOUIS RAMS						
	1	2	3	4	FINAL	
New Orleans	0	14	7	7	28	Record: (9–0)
St. Louis	0	14	3	6	23	Record: (1–8)

ONE OF THE ONLY PLAYMAKERS ON A DISMAL RAMS TEAM, STEVEN JACKSON MANAGED 131 YARDS AND A SCORE BUT WAS BATTERED ALL DAY BY NEW ORLEANS TACKLERS.

LITTLE TO SWEAT ABOUT, FOR ONCE

SAINTS 38, BUCCANEERS 7 • NOVEMBER 22, 2009 • RAYMOND JAMES STADIUM, TAMPA, FLORIDA

For the fourth time in five weeks, the New Orleans Saints fell behind–this time against Tampa Bay. But unlike in previous games, they didn't need a full 60 minutes to overcome their early deficit.

Drew Brees threw three touchdown passes–two to big-play wideout Robert Meachem–and Mike Bell ran for two scores as the Saints won in relatively easy fashion for once, 38–7 on the road in Tampa. The victory improved the Saints to 10–0 and pulled them within one game of clinching a playoff berth.

"I like where we're at. We're 10–0, and we beat a division opponent on the road," coach Sean Payton said. "I thought we got better today."

But New Orleans still fell behind in the first quarter, as Tampa Bay (1–9) drove 95 yards in 12 plays for a touchdown. Rookie quarterback Josh Freeman hit Michael Clayton for an 18-yard score and the Buccaneers led 7–0.

Brees would match that scoring pass with one of his own, a four-yarder to Meachem that made it 7–7. That score stood until rookie cornerback Malcolm Jenkins set up John Carney's 38-yard field goal and a 10–7 Saints lead with his first career interception.

New Orleans scored again just before the half, with Brees connecting with Marques Colston on passes of 16, 20, and 21 yards in a span of four plays before finding Meachem for a 6-yard touchdown and a 17–7 Saints advantage. Meachem's two-score day was his first as a pro and part of a five-week stretch in which he scored a touchdown in every game.

Brees ended the day 19 for 29 for 187 yards and three touchdowns, his fourth three-score game of the season but first since recording four against the New York Giants in Week 6. Despite the absence of all-purpose running back Reggie Bush (knee), the Saints exhibited near-perfect offensive balance, passing for 187 yards and rushing for 183.

"The last four games, we kind of got back to some old habits that we didn't want to, which was the turnovers and negative plays," Brees said. "We needed a game like this, to come out and look sharp in all phases."

New Orleans would score three unanswered touchdowns in the second half, Brees' 11-yard pass to tight end David Thomas and scoring runs of 3 yards and 1 yard by Bell. Pierre Thomas piled up 92 yards rushing on 11 carries, while Bell added 75 yards on 13 carries.

DREW BREES WAS ALL SMILES AFTER ONE OF HIS MOST EFFICIENT PERFORMANCES OF THE SEASON. HE WAS A PERFECT FIVE-FOR-FIVE IN THE RED ZONE AND THREW THREE TOUCHDOWNS AGAINST THE OVERMATCHED TAMPA SECONDARY.

Thomas enjoyed his best day as a Saint with four catches for 66 yards. The former Texas standout was acquired in a preseason trade with New England after back-up tight end Billy Miller was lost for the season due to injury.

After his early success, Tampa Bay's Freeman looked every bit the rookie. The Bucs' top draft pick out of Kansas State finished the game 17 for 33 for 126 yards and one touchdown, but three interceptions.

Jenkins, middle linebacker Jonathan Vilma, and reserve safety Chris Reis each came up with interceptions, and Scott Fujita and Will Smith both had sacks. Tampa Bay totaled just 219 yards of offense, 124 after its opening scoring drive.

"We knew how potent their offense was, and we knew that really the best defense was our offense being able to sustain drives," Freeman said. "The tough thing is that only lasted our first drive."

With Tampa Bay out of the way, New Orleans could finally look ahead to a Monday night showdown against three-time Super Bowl New England in the Superdome, a game sure to provide the Saints with a great measuring stick. Adding to the intrigue was that with a victory and a loss by the Atlanta Falcons, the Saints could clinch the NFC South Division title with five games still to play.

"We're going to play in a lot of big games, and this is a big game because it's the 11th game on our schedule," Payton said. "We know it's a good team that we're playing. We've been on the road for a couple of weeks and are coming back home, but I think we've been able to do that and not just give that lip service. We have to improve a lot from this past week. We have some things we have to clean up." ❧

NEW ORLEANS SAINTS AT TAMPA BAY BUCCANEERS						
	1	2	3	4	FINAL	
New Orleans	7	10	14	7	38	Record: (10–0)
Tampa Bay	7	0	0	0	7	Record: (1–9)

PIERRE THOMAS BREAKS A TACKLE TO GET TO THE SECOND LEVEL. THOMAS AND MIKE BELL COMBINED FOR 163 YARDS ON THE GROUND WITH TWO TOUCHDOWNS TO BALANCE THE NEW ORLEANS OFFENSE.

REMOVING ALL DOUBT

SAINTS 38, PATRIOTS 17 • NOVEMBER 30, 2009 • LOUISIANA SUPERDOME, NEW ORLEANS

Any remaining skeptics probably left the room for good following the New Orleans Saints' Monday night massacre of the New England Patriots on the final day of November. New Orleans proved once and for all it belonged among the NFL's elite, routing the league's model franchise before a national television audience. Drew Brees threw five touchdown passes to as many different receivers—including three in a 21-point second quarter—as the Saints clinched a playoff berth and improved to 11–0 with a 38–17 victory at a raucous Louisiana Superdome.

"This is a big, big win," Saints coach Sean Payton said. "Obviously all of us in this organization have a lot of respect for the things the Patriots have accomplished. We knew this was going to be an electric atmosphere we were playing in and I'm certainly glad we had the crowd behind us. They were awesome."

The Saints rolled up 480 yards of total offense—including 367 through the air—against the Patriots, who have won three Super Bowls this decade. New Orleans intercepted New England quarterback Tom Brady twice, sacked him twice, and knocked him down seven times.

Brees, meanwhile, finished the night 18 for 23 for 371 yards and five scores, with no interceptions. It was one of his most efficient performances of the year, and one off the season-high six touchdowns he threw

against Detroit in the season-opener.

"Drew was special," Payton said. "Let's just say he's playing really well. It was a great job by him. Magnificent."

After New Orleans got John Carney's 30-yard field goal on the game's opening possession, New England (7–4) drove 80 yards in 14 plays to take the lead. Laurence Maroney ran 4 yards for a touchdown on fourth-and-1, putting the Patriots up 7–3 with 3:34 to play in the first.

That would be New England's only lead, as New Orleans scored on all three of its drives in the second quarter. Pierre Thomas set the tone with a 26-yard run on the final play of the first quarter, then scored the Saints' first touchdown on an 18-yard screen pass from Brees for a 10-–7 lead with 12:55 left in the half.

After the Patriots punted on their next drive, the Saints went for the jugular. Brees found Devery Henderson open near midfield and the fleet-footed receiver did the rest, racing for a 75-yard touchdown to put New Orleans up 17–7.

New England answered with Stephen Gostkowski's 36-yard field goal to pull within seven, but New Orleans reached the end zone again on Brees' 38-yard scoring strike to Robert Meachem to go on top 24–10. Gostkowski missed a 50-yard field goal attempt late in

A BIG PART OF DREW BREES' 371-YARD DAY, MARQUES COLSTON CAUGHT A TEAM-HIGH FOUR BALLS FOR 121 YARDS AND A TOUCHDOWN. HERE, HE IS SPRINTING AWAY FROM THE PATRIOTS ON HIS LONGEST GAIN OF THE DAY, A 68-YARD CATCH-AND-RUN.

PIERRE THOMAS HAD YET
ANOTHER SOLID OUTING ON
THE GROUND, AVERAGING
NEARLY SIX YARDS PER
CARRY. THOMAS AND MIKE
BELL COMBINED FOR 114
YARDS AGAINST ONE OF
THE AFC'S MOST STOUT
RUN DEFENSES.

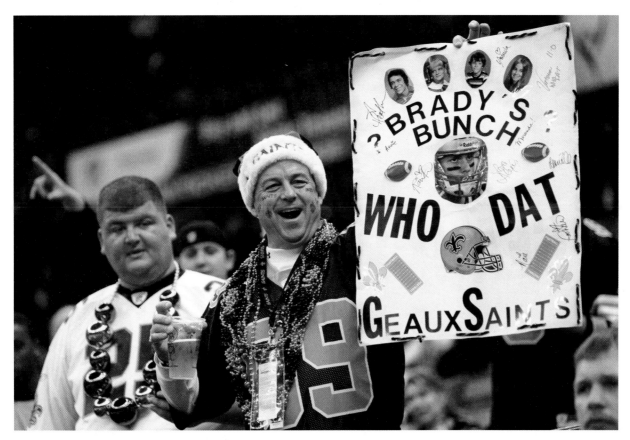

the half, and the two-touchdown lead stood up through the break.

New England got with seven on Maroney's 2-yard run early in the third quarter, but Brees and company responded again. This time it was a 2-yard touchdown pass to little-used tight end Darnell Dinkins, putting the Saints on top 31–17 with 9:02 left in the third.

"We were able to accomplish something offensively tonight that was pretty special," said Brees, who finished with a perfect passer rating of 158.3.

New England's last chance to get back in the game ended when the Patriots turned the ball over on downs at the New Orleans 10 late in the third quarter. The Saints completed the scoring on Brees' 20-yard touchdown pass to Marques Colston with 7:49 to play.

Moments later, Darren Sharper intercepted Brady for the Saints' third forced turnover of the game. The other two came from unlikely sources—a forced fumble by defensive tackle Sedrick Ellis, who had missed four games with a knee injury, and an interception by Mike McKenzie, signed off the street as a free agent a week prior.

"There's obviously a big gap between us," said Brady, who was pulled from the game following Sharper's interception. "It wasn't nearly as competitive as we all were expecting.

"There's a reason why they are 11–0," Brady said. "They played really well and we didn't play up to their level."

For the rest of the NFL, the Saints' level was getting all the more rarified. ❧

NEW ORLEANS SAINTS VS. NEW ENGLAND PATRIOTS						
	1	2	3	4	FINAL	
New England	7	3	7	0	17	Record: (7–4)
New Orleans	3	21	7	7	38	Record: (11–0)

(OPPOSITE) NEW ENGLAND QUARTERBACK TOM BRADY AND COACH BILL BELICHICK COULD ONLY SIT AND WATCH WITH EVERYONE ELSE AS THE SAINTS MANHANDLED THE PATRIOTS. (ABOVE) FANS ENJOYED BEARING WITNESS TO THE ASCENSION OF THE SAINTS OVER THE PATRIOTS IN PRIMETIME.

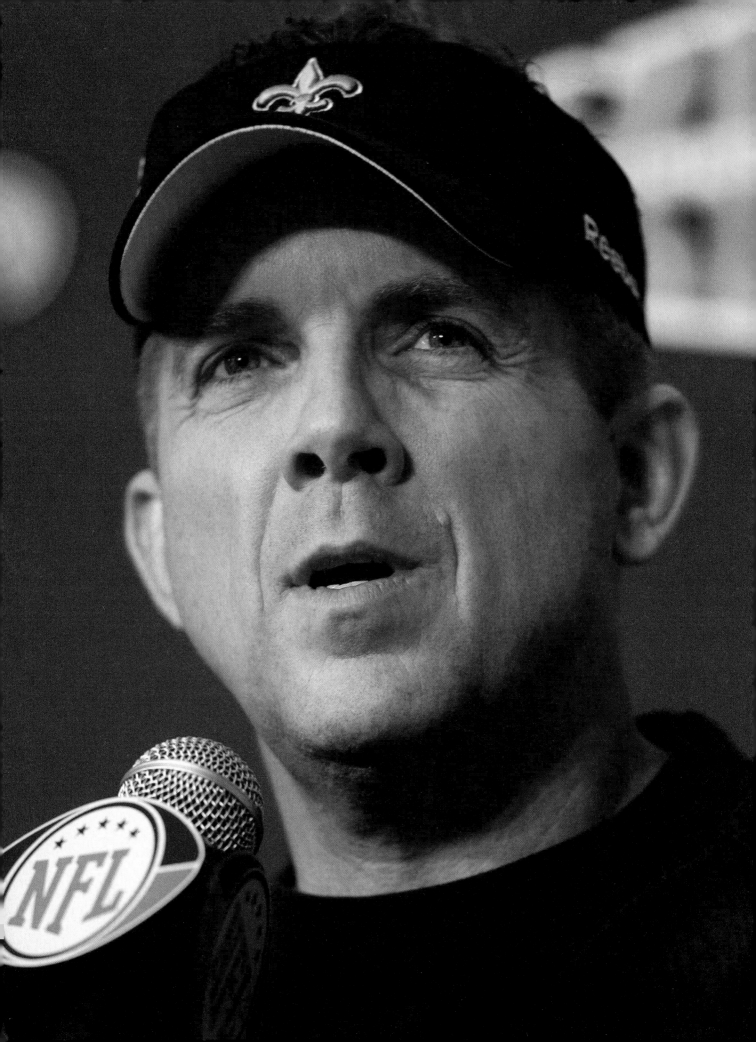

Saints' Payton a Quarterback Guru

Wherever Sean Payton goes, passing numbers are sure to rise. Payton has been an NFL assistant or head coach for 13 years, and in the last 10 of those his starting quarterback has passed for more than 3,000 yards. His quarterbacks have topped the 4,000-yard mark five times, including four straight such performances by the Saints' Drew Brees since Payton took over as head coach before the 2006 season.

Payton's work with quarterbacks, from Kerry Collins to Drew Bledsoe to Tony Romo to Brees, is his calling card and the biggest reason he's the most successful coach in Saints history. He's responsible for four of the franchise's five all-time playoff wins, including the Super Bowl XLIV championship against the Indianapolis Colts.

"I always knew he'd be a good head coach," said Romo, whom Payton groomed during his tenure with the Cowboys (2003–05). "He has the mental makeup and he has the understanding of continuing to get better. I think that's what makes great players and great coaches, is understanding and improvement always being there and continually striving for that. Sean's a guy like that. He's committed to what he's doing and his execution and approach.… He's always had a good mind for football."

Like Romo, the 46-year-old Payton first made his name as a quarterback at tiny Eastern Illinois University, where he led his team to the Division I-AA quarterfinals in 1986. After a brief foray in professional football, Payton spent nine years as a college assistant coach before joining the Philadelphia Eagles as quarterbacks coach in 1997.

He spent two years with the Eagles, then four with the New York Giants, the last three as offensive coordinator (including a Super Bowl run in 2000). Then it was three years in Dallas as assistant head coach/quarterbacks coach before the Saints came calling in 2006.

Through the years, Payton has worked alongside some of the most successful coaches in recent NFL history, including Bill Parcells, Andy Reid, and Tom Coughlin. He said he's always kept his mouth shut and his eyes and ears open.

"I've been fortunate to be around a lot of real talented coaches and watched," Payton said. "Any time you're coming up young in the profession, you pay attention to the guy that's you're working with on the staff with and working for as head coaches. And I've been fortunate in that regard. "

Since coming to New Orleans, however, Payton has found an offensive soulmate in Saints quarterback

THE FIERY SEAN PAYTON PROVIDED AN INSTANT TURNAROUND WHEN HE TOOK THE SAINTS' COACHING JOB. HE TOOK A TEAM THAT HAD GONE 3–13 THE YEAR BEFORE AND—BUOYED BY ONE OF THE NFL'S BEST OFFENSES— LED THEM TO AN NFC SOUTH TITLE AND A BERTH IN THE NFC CHAMPIONSHIP GAME.

Drew Brees. Payton hand-picked the former San Diego Charger to be his quarterback during the 2005–06 off-season, and the two have taken the New Orleans team to new heights offensively.

Brees has passed for at least 4,388 yards and 26 touchdowns in each of his four seasons with the Saints, including 5,069 yards (second all-time in NFL history) and 34 scores in 2008. New Orleans has led the NFL in scoring each of the last two seasons, something Brees ascribes to the almost-eerie sense of simpatico between him and Payton.

"I'd say pretty much all the time we're seeing the same thing," Brees told The Times-Picayune of New Orleans in January. "During the week, as we're going through meetings, we can put the pass pictures on the overhead projector and he's talking, 'Hey, the first third down inside the 20, this is what (play) I'm getting to.' Or the minute we cross the 50, or the first play of the second half, or the first goal-line play, 'I'm dialing this up.' So, sure enough, you get in the game and you encounter that situation. And in my mind I reflect back to what he's said, and sure enough, that's the play call that comes in.

"That's when you know you're on the same page as the play caller, which is a great thing. It obviously helps us be successful."

Though Romo didn't become the Cowboys' starting quarterback until after Payton left for New Orleans, he credits his old mentor for a large portion of his success. (Romo is a two-time Pro Bowler.) It's that same work ethic that has lifted the Saints to a championship level, he said.

"Sean's a very bright guy," Romo said. "He understands people. He understands football. He's got a good mind for things. He just knows how to continually look at improving and getting better for year to year and week to week and I think it just shows that obviously the season's been great for them. They had some bumpy roads along the way (last season). But they stayed the course, continued to improve and get better and try to continue with what they did this year. That's just part of the process. Sean understands the bigger picture and he keeps going forward." ∝

HOISTING THE GEORGE HALAS TROPHY FOLLOWING THE HISTORIC WIN OVER THE VIKINGS, SEAN PAYTON KNEW THAT WHILE HE HAD ACCOMPLISHED ONE OF HIS GOALS, THE VINCE LOMBARDI TROPHY STILL BECKONED.

ANOTHER GREEN ESCAPE
ANOTHER GREAT ESCAPE

SAINTS 33, REDSKINS 30 (OT) • DECEMBER 6, 2009 • FEDEX FIELD, LANDOVER, MARYLAND

Of all the close victories the New Orleans Saints had in 2009, perhaps none—the NFC Championship Game included—featured as wild a finish as the 33–30 overtime win at Washington on December 6. The Saints pulled out their 12th straight victory to start the season thanks to an all-time failure by the opposing kicker, a clutch drive by Drew Brees, a couple of huge defensive plays, and one fortunate instant replay review. But in the end, the win counted the same as all the others, and New Orleans had clinched the NFC South title.

"I almost feel speechless, but that's a big win," Saints running back Mike Bell said. "I really have nothing to say. Our team has so much heart, we work so hard, and it started from the offseason, this is just a special team. We played a good team out there and they never gave up. We don't want to take anything from them, but our team is special."

New Orleans trailed by seven headed into the final two minutes, with Washington in possession of the ball at the Saints' 4-yard line and lining up for a potential game-clinching field goal. But Shaun Suisham's 23-yard attempt sliced wide right and the Saints clung to life.

Given a second chance, Brees wasted no time driving his team for the tying score. The Saints went 80 yards in just 33 seconds, the final 53 yards on a touchdown pass from Brees to Robert Meachem that tied the game after Garrett Hartley's extra point.

The Saints' Jonathan Vilma then intercepted the ball right back and New Orleans had a chance to win it regulation. But Hartley's 58-yard attempt was well short and the game went to overtime.

Washington won the overtime coin toss, but New Orleans' big-play defense forced a turnover on just the third play of the extra period. Redskins' quarterback Jason Campbell threw a short pass to fullback Mike Sellers, who appeared to fumble after a hit from the Saints' Chris McAlister, who also recovered the ball.

On-field officials ruled that Sellers was down by contact, but the replay official overruled him, giving the Saints the ball on the Washington 37-yard line. Three first downs moved the ball to the 1, and Hartley—who beat out regular kicker John Carney for the job during the week of practice—came on and drilled an 18-yard game-winner.

"I definitely believe in destiny, and I believe in karma and what goes around comes around," said Brees, who passed for a season-high 419 yards in the

THE SAINTS GANG UP TO DROP WASHINGTON'S ANTWAAN RANDLE-EL. THEY HAD TROUBLE ALL DAY SLOWING THE WASHINGTON ATTACK, BUT ONCE THE SAINTS GOT CLOSE IN THE FOURTH QUARTER, THEY MANAGED TO CLOSE THE DOOR AND GIVE THE OFFENSE AN OPPORTUNITY TO TIE.

game. "We have been on the other side of this deal probably too many times, maybe its our time that we start catching some of the breaks and start being the team that wins them like this in the end. I feel like if you continue to do things the right way then good things happen to you."

For the game's beginning, almost nothing went right for the Saints, however. Washington led by 10 points at three different times in the game, including at 30–20 entering the final seven minutes.

A key moment came just before halftime, with Washington leading 17–10 after the second of three Campbell touchdown passes. Brees was intercepted at the Washington 30-yard line by diving Redskins safety Kareem Moore, who got to his feet and returned the ball to the 44.

But Meachem swooped in for the tackle and pulled the ball away in one motion, racing to the end zone to tie the game at 17. Replay officials upheld the score, and New Orleans went to the locker room with momentum for the first time all day.

"We've been working on (ball-stripping) drills like that since we started in (offseason workouts)," said Meachem, who caught eight passes for 142 yards in the game. "The defense always works on those types of drills."

The Redskins scored the first 10 points of the second half to go back on top 27–17, but New Orleans outscored Washington 16–3 the rest of the way and escaped with the victory. The Saints won again despite allowing 455 yards and being penalized seven times for 102 yards, thanks to more than a few wild twists and turns.

"Crazy plays," Vilma said. "When you're hot, you're hot. And sometimes it's better to be lucky than good." ∞

NEW ORLEANS SAINTS AT WASHINGTON REDSKINS

	1	2	3	4	OT	FINAL	
New Orleans	0	17	3	10	3	33	Record: (12–0)
Washington	10	7	10	3	0	30	Record: (3–9)

ROBERT MEACHEM GALLOPS INTO THE END ZONE WITH 1:13 LEFT ON THE CLOCK TO EVEN THE GAME AT 30. THE RECEIVER HAD A BANNER DAY, RECORDING EIGHT CATCHES FOR 142 YARDS, INCLUDING THE SCORE.

VILMA VANQUISHES ATLANTA

SAINTS 26, FALCONS 23 • DECEMBER 13, 2009 • GEORGIA DOME, ATLANTA, GEORGIA

Jonathan Vilma proved in Week 14 that Darren Sharper isn't the only big-play veteran on the New Orleans Saints' defense. Vilma, the team's Pro Bowl middle linebacker, thwarted the Atlanta Falcons twice in the fourth quarter—once on an interception and once on a fourth-down stop—as the Saints set a team record with their 13th victory of the season, 26–23 in the Georgia Dome. The victory kept the Saints undefeated and completed a season-sweep of their arch-rivals for the third time in four years.

"Those two defensive plays (by Vilma) were important," Saints coach Sean Payton said. "They helped secure the victory, and even though we struggled at times, those plays combined with our offense's ability to score the touchdowns earlier in the game helped the lead hold up. It's never easy winning in this league, and it's always a tough game when you play the Falcons. They fought really hard today and had great effort, and we were fortunate to make the plays when we needed them the most."

Garrett Hartley's 38-yard field goal gave the Saints a three-point lead with 4:42 to play, setting up Vilma's late heroics. The sixth-year man from Miami intercepted Chris Redman's second-down pass at the Saints'

43 and returned the ball to the 32 with 3:53 left.

But New Orleans couldn't run out the clock and gave the ball back to Atlanta at the 15-yard line when holder Mark Brunell's fake-field-goal pass fell incomplete with 2:07 remaining. Redman drove the Falcons as far as the Saints' 46, where Vilma stopped fullback Jason Snelling a yard short of a first down on fourth-and-2 and gave New Orleans the ball back to run out the clock.

"We always want them to put it on our shoulders at the end of the game," said Vilma, who ended with a game-high seven tackles in addition to his interception.

Prior to Vilma's late heroics, it was a ho-hum day for the Saints. Despite entering the day with a chance to wrap up a first-round bye in the playoffs, New Orleans looked slightly off-kilter against a pesky Falcons team.

The Falcons were playing without starting quarterback Matt Ryan and Pro Bowl running back Michael Turner, but still outgained the high-powered Saints 392 yards to 391. Redman passed for 303 yards and a touchdown, leading back-to-back scoring drives that helped Atlanta erase a 23–9 deficit in the final quarter-and-a-half.

Redman hit Michael Jenkins for 50 yards and

JONATHAN VILMA EXPRESSES HIMSELF AFTER THE SAINTS STOPPED THE ATLANTA FALCONS ON FOURTH DOWN LATE IN THE GAME.

Snelling ran for a four-yard touchdown, tying the game with 12:56 to play. The Saints answered with a 16-play drive for Hartley's go-ahead field goal, and dismissed any trepidation about so many close calls after Vilma's two big plays clinched the victory.

"Why would we be concerned? We're 13–0," Vilma said. "You're not going to get many blowout wins in the NFL."

On a day when the Saints rushed for only 67 yards, quarterback Drew Brees carried the offense once again. He completed 31-of-40 passes for 296 yards and three touchdowns, including two to Reggie Bush. Brees' first TD to Bush erased an early 6–3 lead for the Falcons, and his 3-yarder to Marques Colston put New Orleans up 16–6 late in the second quarter. Hartley missed the extra point, allowing Atlanta's Matt Bryant to tie make it 16–9 with a 27-yard field goal on the final play of the half.

Brees hit Bush for a 21-yard score to make it 23–9 early in the third quarter, but the Saints couldn't get into the end zone again, leaving the door open for the Atlanta rally, Hartley's game-winner and the Vilma-led late defensive stands. Bush, who played sparingly the previous week against Washington after missing two games with a knee injury, recorded a season-high six receptions to go with his two touchdowns.

Once again, the win wasn't pretty, but it still went down the same in the "W" column. And unlike some previous games, the Saints won this one with defense. "No matter what the situation, we always feel like we have an opportunity to win," Brees said. "Whether it's our offense, defense, or special teams, somehow we're going to find a way to win the game." ⌾

NEW ORLEANS SAINTS AT ATLANTA FALCONS						
	1	2	3	4	FINAL	
New Orleans	3	13	7	3	26	Record: (13–0)
Atlanta	6	3	7	7	23	Record: (6–7)

WITH A STEP ON HIS DEFENDER, MARQUES COLSTON REACHES OUT TO CATCH ONE HIS SIX PASSES FROM DREW BREES. HE SCORED A TOUCHDOWN AND SAW HIS TEAM RUN OUT TO A 23–9 LEAD BEFORE THEY NEEDED A LATE FIELD GOAL TO PULL OUT THE WIN.

NOBODY'S PERFECT

COWBOYS 24, SAINTS 17 • DECEMBER 19, 2009 • LOUISIANA SUPERDOME, NEW ORLEANS

The New Orleans Saints couldn't protect quarterback Drew Brees in Week 15 against the Dallas Cowboys, and that meant the end of their quest for a perfect season. The Cowboys sacked Brees four times—forcing him to fumble twice—and held New Orleans to a season-low in points on their way to a 24–17 victory in the Superdome, dropping the Saints to 13-1. New Orleans rallied from a 21-point deficit with two fourth-quarter touchdowns, but DeMarcus Ware's sack and forced fumble on Brees with six seconds left ended any hopes of another miracle comeback for the Saints.

"They've got a good defense and deserve a lot of credit," Brees said. "For us, it was one of those nights where things weren't quite clicking. Unfortunately, we didn't handle (the pass rush) very well. We weren't very good on third downs tonight. That's not going to score you many points."

New Orleans couldn't establish a rhythm all night, going without an offensive touchdown for the first three quarters. Dallas, meanwhile, played some of its best football of the year, scoring touchdowns on its first two drives of the game to take a 14–0 lead after one quarter.

Following a Saints punt on the game's opening possession, it took the Cowboys (9–5) just five plays to get into the end zone. On first down from the New Orleans 49, quarterback Tony Romo found receiver Miles Austin behind the Saints defense for a touchdown and a 7–0 Dallas advantage with 11:24 left in the first.

The Saints went three-and-out on their next possession and Dallas scored another touchdown, using a 26-yard pass from Romo to Austin to get into the red zone. Marion Barber crashed over left guard for the touchdown and the Cowboys led by two touchdowns less than 10 minutes into the game.

"They simply executed," Saints cornerback Tracy Porter said. "They executed on our misfortunes. We were out of position on a few plays. They have a really good offense and they capitalized on our mistakes."

New Orleans finally put together a scoring drive midway through the second quarter, but could manage only Garrett Hartley's 34-yard field goal to pull within 14–3. Dallas answered with Nick Folk's 44-yarder to make it a 14-point game once again going into the half.

Dallas came right out guns blazing again in the third quarter, driving 74 yards in 13 plays for another touchdown. Barber converted a third-and-1 from the 6 with a 4-yard run, then ran the ball in two plays

later to put the Cowboys on top 24–3.

Dallas' defense continued to make life miserable for Brees the rest of the third quarter, sacking him on back-to-back plays at one stretch. Heading into the final period, New Orleans still trailed by three scores.

The offense finally got going early in the fourth, as Brees completed 6-of-7 passes on an 80-yard scoring drive capped by Mike Bell's 1-yard touchdown. Following a Dallas punt, Brees led an 85-yard march ending in a 7-yard touchdown strike to Lance Moore to improbably pull the Saints within 24–17 with eight minutes to play.

Dallas then went on a long, time-consuming drive of its own, but couldn't put the game away when Folk's 24-yard field goal attempt clanged off the right upright and fell harmlessly to the ground. That gave the Saints one last chance, and Brees moved them as far as the Dallas 42 before Ware beat tackle Jermon Bushrod

around left end for the game-deciding turnover.

Romo, who passed for 312 yards in the game, then took a knee to end the game and send a record Superdome crowd of 70,213 home in stunned silence. Romo's opposite number was left to lament what might have been had the Saints pulled off the perfect season.

"That's disappointing," Brees said. "You don't know how many chances you're going to get at that. That's tough. I feel like we've fought so hard to get where we're at. You just feel like we deserved it and the city deserved it and the organization deserved it. We wanted to make it happen for all of them." ❧

NEW ORLEANS SAINTS VS. DALLAS COWBOYS						
	1	2	3	4	FINAL	
Dallas	14	3	7	0	24	Record: (9–5)
New Orleans	0	3	0	14	17	Record: (13–1)

SAFETY PIERSON PRIOLEAU REFLECTS THE TEAM'S ATTITUDE IN A LOSS AGAINST THE DALLAS COWBOYS.

SNATCHING DEFEAT FROM VICTORY

BUCCANEERS 20, SAINTS 17 (OT) • DECEMBER 27, 2009 • LOUISIANA SUPERDOME, NEW ORLEANS

The New Orleans Saints provided a textbook example of how not to close out a game in Week 16 against Tampa Bay. Playing in the final home game of the regular season, New Orleans blew a two-touchdown lead in the fourth quarter, missed a gimme field goal at the end of regulation, then lost in overtime. The 20–17 defeat to the lowly Buccaneers left the suddenly ice-cold Saints with their second straight defeat after beginning the season with 13 consecutive victories.

"That's something we've got to work on," Saints receiver Robert Meachem said. "Start from scratch, see what we did wrong. We've just got to take the coaching, the criticism, and go with it. A loss is a loss, no matter how you lose it."

The only good news of the weekend came the next day, when Chicago beat Minnesota to hand the Vikings their fourth loss of the season. That meant the Saints, who could finish no worse than 13–3, would have home-field advantage throughout the NFC playoffs.

But New Orleans could have clinched the No. 1 seed in front of the home folks by playing better down the stretch. The Saints led 17–3 as late as the 13:14 mark of the fourth quarter, when Carnell Williams raced around left end for a 23-yard touchdown run to pull the Buccaneers within seven.

New Orleans turned the ball over on its next possession (though Tampa Bay didn't score) and committed an even worse sin following an unfruitful drive as the clock ticked inside three minutes. The Bucs' Micheal Spurlock returned a punt 77 yards for a touchdown and suddenly the game was tied with 2:41 to play. "It's a punt return," Saints coach Sean Payton said. "We've got to get off blocks and cover it and do the fundamentals of covering a punt."

Said Bucs coach Raheem Morris, "(Spurlock) provided us the play that put us in this thing. He gave us life. He did a great job."

The Saints still had a chance to win the game, and Brees drove them 50 yards in eight plays to move into Tampa Bay territory. His third-down pass to Meachem put the ball on the 19, and on came Hartley with five seconds to play.

New Orleans had given Hartley a full vote of confidence by releasing veteran back-up John Carney during the week, but the second-year man failed to deliver the game-winner. His 38-yard attempt went wide left and the game went to overtime.

"I felt great going out there, just an opportunity to win another game and give us home-field advantage in the playoffs," said Hartley, whose miss was the first in 22 career attempts from inside 50 yards. "I kind of rushed myself a little bit. It was all me, the snap and hold were great; I just rushed myself.

"Knowing I let my team down is the worst thing. It's definitely humbling. You have to learn from these experiences in order to prevail on the next one."

New Orleans never touched the ball in the extra period, as Tampa Bay ran the ball on 11 consecutive plays—10 of those by Williams, who rushed for 129 yards on 24 carries in the game—to move into field goal range. With 9:06 left in overtime, the Buccaneers' Connor Barth drilled a 47-yarder to give Tampa Bay the victory.

Brees completed 32-of-37 passes for 258 yards, including a 30-yard touchdown pass to Meachem. Pierre Thomas rushed for an 8-yard score and Hartley hit a 28-yard field goal to give the Saints a 17–0 lead

midway through the second quarter. But that would be all the scoring for New Orleans, which was held without a point after halftime for the first time all year.

"The fact is we need to play better," Brees said. "I don't feel like we've played our best football in a while and there's definitely some things that need to be corrected.

"You always find out more about a team when you start facing adversity. This is just yet another one of those situations that I feel we have the right character, the right type of leadership to bounce back from and help us become stronger going into the playoffs." ℘

NEW ORLEANS SAINTS VS. TAMPA BAY BUCCANEERS							
	1	2	3	4	OT	FINAL	
Tampa Bay	0	3	0	14	3	20	Record: (3–12)
New Orleans	14	3	0	0	0	17	Record: (13–2)

MIKE BELL SCRATCHES AHEAD FOR YARDS. THE SAINTS GOT PRODUCTIVE CARRIES OUT OF FIVE DIFFERENT RUNNERS FOR 124 YARDS TOTAL, GIVING THE SAINTS A CHANCE TO TIE AT THE END BEFORE GARRETT HARTLEY'S LAST-SECOND FIELD-GOAL TRY HOOKED LEFT.

LIVING TO FIGHT ANOTHER DAY

PANTHERS 23, SAINTS 10 • JANUARY 3, 2010 • BANK OF AMERICA STADIUM, CHARLOTTE, NORTH CAROLINA

With the No. 1 seed for the NFC playoffs already clinched and the hopes of a perfect season already dashed, the only question heading into New Orleans' regular-season finale at Carolina was how much, if at all, the Saints' stars would participate. As it turned out, quarterback Drew Brees and several other key players never left the sideline as the Saints closed out the regular portion of the schedule with a 23–10 loss to the Panthers. While heading into the postseason on a three-game losing streak was a less-than-ideal scenario, New Orleans coach Sean Payton said his team had more important things to think about.

"The idea of…having your quarterback not healthy for a divisional playoff game doesn't sound real appealing to me," Payton said. "The key now is to get ourselves mentally and physically refreshed and ready (for the postseason)."

The week began with the naming of five New Orleans players to the Pro Bowl: Brees, offensive guard Jahri Evans, offensive tackle Jonathan Stinchcomb, middle linebacker Jonathan Vilma, and free safety Darren Sharper. Center Jonathan Goodwin and strong safety Roman Harper would later be

named to the game as injury replacements, though none would ultimately play in the game because of the Saints' Super Bowl berth.

Tight end Jeremy Shockey did not dress and running back Reggie Bush played only sparingly, but despite Payton's best efforts the Saints were not able to avoid injury. Starting defensive end Charles Grant, the team's longest-tenured player, was lost for the playoffs with a torn triceps muscle suffered in the second quarter.

Instead of Brees, it was veteran back-up Mark Brunell who earned the start under center against Carolina. Making his first start since the 2006 season with Washington, Brunell completed just 15-of-29 throws for 102 yards and an interception as the Saints managed season-lows in points and total yards (213). "Would I have loved it if we came out here and scored 41 today? I mean, yeah," said Brees, who had a string 79 consecutive starts broken. "But is it worth the risk?"

Carolina–long eliminated from the playoff race but gunning for a break-even season after losing their first three games and four of their first six–took control early against New Orleans. Jonathan Stewart burst off right tackle for a 67-yard touchdown on the game's second play, giving the Panthers a 7–0 lead

that would stand up the rest of the day.

Garrett Hartley hit a 35-yard field goal in the second quarter to pull New Orleans within 7–3, but Carolina scored 10 points in a 13-second span at the end of the half to all but put the game way. First came Matt Moore's 30-yard touchdown pass to Dwayne Jarrett, which made it 14–3 with 13 seconds left in the half. The Saints' Courtney Roby then fumbled the ensuing kickoff at his own 23, and John Kasay came on for a 41-yard field goal as time expired to put Carolina on top 17–3 at the break.

The second half saw little drama, with all the scoring in the third quarter. Kasay hit a pair of field goals to put Carolina on top 23–3, and Lynell Hamilton bounded in a 1-yard touchdown to finally put New Orleans in the end zone with seven seconds left in the period to complete the scoring.

Despite scoring only 10 points against Carolina and a combined 44 in their final three regular-season games, New Orleans ended up as the league's top-scoring team with a club-record 510 points. Though he played in just 15 games, Brees ended up leading the league in touchdown passes (34), completion percentage (70.6) and quarterback rating (109.6), with all three numbers marking career-highs.

Also recording career- and NFL-highs in multiple categories was free safety Darren Sharper: interceptions (9), return yards (376), and touchdowns (3). Wide receiver Marques Colston led a balanced New Orleans passing game with 70 receptions, 1,074 yards, and nine touchdowns.

Sharper and offensive guard Jahri Evans earned first-team All-Pro recognition following the season, while Brees was picked for the second team. ⸙

NEW ORLEANS SAINTS AT CAROLINA PANTHERS						
	1	2	3	4	FINAL	
New Orleans	0	3	7	0	10	Record: (13–3)
Carolina	7	10	6	0	23	Record: (8–8)

WITH STARTER DREW BREES ON THE BENCH, MARK BRUNELL COMPLETED 15 PASSES TO NINE DIFFERENT RECEIVERS, INCLUDING THIS ONE TO MARQUES COLSTON. THE SAINTS AVERAGED ONLY 3.5 YARDS PER PLAY IN THE RUNNING GAME AND MUSTERED JUST 213 YARDS OF TOTAL OFFENSE.

RESTORING THEIR MOJO

SAINTS 45, CARDINALS 14 • NFC DIVISIONAL PLAYOFF • JANUARY 16, 2009 • LOUISIANA SUPERDOME, NEW ORLEANS

Perhaps the trend-spotters should have paid more attention the full body of work when handicapping the New Orleans Saints' NFC divisional playoff match-up with the Arizona Cardinals. The Saints ended the regular season as one of the coldest teams in the NFL, losing their final three games to not only put a damper on a 13–0 start but also leave doubts they could flip the switch back on for the postseason. No team, let alone a conference's top seed, that ended the season on a three-game losing streak had ever reached the Super Bowl.

The Cardinals, meanwhile, were red-hot, having out-gunned Green Bay in the wild-card round while the Saints sat and waited with a first-round bye. Arizona also boasted an offense led by quarterback Kurt Warner and wide receiver Larry Fitzgerald, players who had sparked the Cardinals to a Super Bowl just one season before.

Ten seconds in it looked as if the Saints' skeptics might be right, as Arizona's Tim Hightower raced 70 yards for a touchdown on the game's first play. The rest of the day belonged to New Orleans, however, as the Saints pounded the Cardinals 45–14 to advance to the NFC Championship Game for the second time in four years.

"So much for being rusty," Saints coach Sean

Payton said. "That bye week was critical, getting guys healthy.... I knew we were ready, the way we worked all week and we were confident in what we were going to do."

Following Hightower's first-strike touchdown, New Orleans dominated the rest of the way. The Saints led 21–7 after one quarter and 35–14 at halftime.

The star of the day was New Orleans running back Reggie Bush, who totaled 217 yards and two touchdowns rushing, receiving, and on returns. He gave the Saints a commanding first-quarter lead with a brilliant 49-yard touchdown run, then provided the capper with an 83-yard punt return for a score in the third quarter. "I knew I was going to get a lot of opportunities today to make plays and just be a difference-maker for my team," Bush said. "I just tried to make the most of it every time I had the ball."

But Bush had plenty of credit to share. Drew Brees passed for 247 yards and three touchdowns, one each to Jeremy Shockey, Devery Henderson, and Marques Colston (who led all receivers with six catches for 83 yards).

The Saints defense also forced a pair of turnovers—an interception by defensive end Will Smith and a fumble recovery by safety Darren Sharper—and kept Fitzgerald and the Cardinals' dynamic receiving corps

WILL SMITH GETS THE CROWD EXCITED DURING THE DIVISIONAL PLAYOFF GAME IN NEW ORLEANS AGAINST THE ARIZONA CARDINALS.

MARQUES COLSTON SNARES THE BALL OUT OF THE AIR WHILE ARIZONA CARDINALS MICHAEL ADAMS CAN ONLY WATCH. COLSTON HAD A PRODUCTIVE DAY, RACKING UP 83 YARDS ON SIX CATCHES AND SCORING A THIRD-QUARTER TOUCHDOWN THAT PUT THE GAME OUT OF REACH.

REGGIE BUSH LOOKS BACK AT CARDINALS DEFENDERS LEFT IN HIS WAKE AS HE SCORES A 46-YARD TOUCHDOWN IN THE FIRST QUARTER.

out of the end zone. Though they sacked Kurt Warner only once, they generally made life miserable for the Arizona quarterback by hitting him repeatedly, including when they temporarily knocked him out of the game with a block following Smith's interception.

"It didn't end the way we wanted it to," said Warner, who ended up retiring from football later in the month. "It wasn't nearly as competitive as we wanted it to be, but sometimes you have those days. Today was one of those days for us."

It was all jubilation for the Saints, who found themselves one win from the franchise's first Super Bowl appearance. Payton also answered critics who said he was unwise to rest his starters, rather than go for a streak-snapping victory, in the final regular-season game against Carolina.

Brees certainly appeared fresh, while Shockey shook off a late-season toe injury to catch three passes for 36 yards, including the touchdown. After building such a big lead early, the New Orleans quarterback's thought inevitably drifted to the NFC championship match-up with Minnesota the following week.

"There's been a lot of firsts since Sean Payton has been here in the organization and we want to keep that going," Brees said. "We want to bring this franchise a championship. There's no fan base that deserves a championship more than New Orleans and the Who-dat nation. Just the bond that we have with them is special. They give us strength. They give us motivation, and we want to do it for them." ❧

NEW ORLEANS SAINTS VS. ARIZONA CARDINALS						
	1	2	3	4	SCORE	
Arizona	7	7	0	0	14	Record: (10–7)
New Orleans	21	14	10	0	45	Record: (14–3)

KURT WARNER IS TACKLED BY WILL SMITH AND SEDRICK ELLIS. HE TOOK A BEATING FROM THE SAINTS DEFENSE IN HIS LAST GAME BEFORE RETIRING.

A Little Reggie Goes a Long Way

Reggie Bush came to the New Orleans Saints in 2006 as one of the most-heralded draft picks in franchise history. But three years into Bush's NFL career, many discussions about the former Heisman Trophy winner from Southern California would drop the letter "H" from his last name and replace it with a "T."

Oh, Bush certainly had his moments—such as a four-touchdown outburst against San Francisco his rookie year, a game-winning touchdown and two-point conversion against Atlanta in 2007, and two punt returns for touchdowns against Minnesota in 2008. But what Bush lacked was the every-down and every-game consistency worthy of a player considered the Saints' franchise savior when he was taken with the No. 2 overall pick in the first season following Hurricane Katrina.

Unless Bush and the Saints' could figure out a way to better utilize his talents, the whispers about him being a "bust" would continue to grow. For his part, Bush seems immune to the pressure.

"First of all, I don't think about pressure, because I don't think it's pressure to play in a football game," Bush said. "I think pressure is when you have to fly to Afghanistan and defend your country and deal with live bullets. That's pressure. This is fun. That's what I

try to remember, just to have fun and try not to think about pressure. Working on my assignments, doing what I have to do, being a difference maker and doing whatever I can."

Nevertheless, Bush entered the 2009 season with a renewed sense of purpose. Job No. 1 was improving on his yards-per-carry average, which had never topped 3.8 yards in his NFL career.

To that end, head coach Sean Payton and offensive coordinator Pete Carmichael Jr. made the decision to take the running-game load off of Bush, using Pierre Thomas and Mike Bell to do the dirty, between-the tackles work. Bush would be used mainly as a change of-pace back in the running game, in addition to his usual role as a third-down receiver out of the backfield.

Bush carried the ball only 70 times, 36 fewer than in 2008, despite playing in four more games. This was also less than half his rookie-year total of 155. On the other hand, his per-carry-average went up to 5.6 nearly two yards better than his previous career-high. Bush did so by altering his running style, becoming intent on getting up-field immediately rather than dancing in the backfield or in the hole. But to Payton, it was more of a natural progression.

"He's a guy that has worked very hard," Payton

Falling forward for extra yards, Reggie Bush has epitomized hard work on the field since being drafted by the Saints. He missed two games in 2009 and had career lows in most statistical categories, but his eight touchdowns all seemed to come at important moments.

said. "Each year he has matured and he's very competitive and looks forward to these big moments and is someone who rises to these opportunities."

Bush also entered the season coming off a serious left-knee injury for the second straight year. He missed the final four games of the 2007 season with a torn posterior cruciate ligament, then went on injured reserve with six weeks left in 2008 with an injury to the same knee that would eventually require microfracture surgery.

Though Bush's microfracture procedure was not considered as serious as the one that derailed Deuce McAllister's career the previous season, Payton was still intent on managing his recovery. He used Bush sparingly during the regular season—even resting him for two games when his knee began to swell—with an eye toward the postseason.

"The key is having your guys at full strength and we did feel like in his case he was completely healthy," Payton said in mid-January. "A few months ago I told him, 'Just keep chopping the wood and keep working hard; you're too explosive of a player.'"

Bush remained as dangerous as ever as a receiver out of the backfield, hauling in 47 passes, good for fifth-best on the team. He didn't make many memorable plays in the return game, that is, until the playoffs.

In the Saints' 45–14 victory over Arizona in the divisional round, Bush returned a punt 83 yards for a touchdown—and also rushed for a 46-yard touchdown on the way to a 217-all-purpose-yard day. Quarterback Drew Brees said it was the Bush performance the Saints' offensive brain trust had been waiting for.

"He's able to do so many things," Brees said. "He's a very versatile player that can obviously run the ball effectively out of the backfield, you can get it to him on the perimeter, throw the ball to him out of the backfield, split him out, throw the ball to him. What he brings in special teams in regards to the return game. When he's on and he's hot, it's fun to watch." ❧

BUSH HAS BEEN A FAN FAVORITE SINCE THE DAY HE WAS DRAFTED—ORDERS WERE PLACED FOR 15,000 BUSH JERSEYS IN THE WEEK AFTER HE WAS SELECTED—AND HE IS SECOND IN THE NFL IN ENDORSEMENTS TO PEYTON MANNING.

NEXT YEAR
FINALLY ARRIVES

SAINTS 31, VIKINGS 28 (OT) • NFC CHAMPIONSHIP GAME • JANUARY 24, 2009 • LOUISIANA SUPERDOME, NEW ORLEANS

Conventional wisdom dictates that one should say as little as possible to a kicker when a game is on the line, lest you put unnecessary thoughts into his head at a time when his mind should be clear and focused. But New Orleans Saints coach Sean Payton wasn't buying into tradition or superstition in overtime of the NFC Championship Game. As Garrett Hartley got set to attempt a 40-yard field goal that could send the Saints their first-ever Super Bowl, Payton called his second-year kicker over to the side.

"I just told him there's a little fleur de lis up there right between both uprights, and I said 'why don't you see if you can hit this fleur de lis dead center?'" Payton said. "'We belong, you are here for a reason, and you are going to hit it through.'"

Hartley of course delivered, kicking the ball straight down the middle to give New Orleans a 31–28 victory over Minnesota. His game-winner came at the end of a wild series of events that saw the Saints emerge victorious despite being on the verge of almost-certain defeat just minutes earlier.

Minnesota had a third-and-10 at the New Orleans 33-yard line with 19 seconds left in regulation, well within kicker Ryan Longwell's range for a game-winning field goal. But the Vikings were called for 12 men in the huddle and penalized five yards, knocking them out of field-goal position and forcing quarterback Brett Favre to pass the ball one more time.

Favre made a crucial error at the most inopportune time for his club, forcing a ball over the middle that was intercepted by New Orleans' Tracy Porter to secure overtime. The Saints' won the toss and drove 39 yards in 10 plays to begin the extra period, ending in Hartley's now-legendary kick, which he said he had envisioned the night before in a phone call with his father in Texas.

"I guess I was off by two yards," said Hartley, who had told his father he'd kick a 42-yarder for the win. "But I knew it as soon as it left my foot. I didn't even see it go through the upright because I turned to hug (holder) Mark (Brunell)."

Prior to the wild finish, the game was shaping up as one that the Saints were very fortunate to be in. Minnesota outgained New Orleans 475 yards to 257, but turned the ball over five times to keep the Saints in contention.

Adrian Peterson scored three touchdowns for Minnesota, including a 2-yarder to tie the game with

DEVERY HENDERSON SKIES TO HAUL IN HIS SECOND-QUARTER TOUCHDOWN PASS FROM NINE YARDS OUT. THE CATCH TIED THE SCORE AT 14, AND THE TWO TEAMS WENT TO THE DRESSING ROOMS AT HALFTIME DEADLOCKED.

DREW BREES FIST PUMPS TO THE FANS AS HE IS INTERVIEWED BY CHRIS MEYERS AFTER THE GAME. BREES THREW THREE TOUCHDOWN PASSES AND THOUGH HE HAD SIGNIFICANTLY FEWER PASSING YARDS THAN BRETT FAVRE, MANAGED NOT TO TURN THE BALL OVER.

DARREN SHARPER CLOSES
IN ON MINNESOTA'S
ADRIAN PETERSON. THE
ALL-PRO BACK HAD 122
YARDS RUSHING AND
SCORED THREE TIMES BUT
PUT THE BALL ON THE
SUPERDOME TURF TWICE.
THE VIKINGS HANDED
THE BALL TO THE SAINTS
THROUGHOUT THE GAME,
LOSING THREE FUMBLES
AND THROWING A PAIR OF
INTERCEPTIONS.

4:22 to play. But the All-Pro also fumbled twice, once inside the Saints' 10 and once inside his own 10 to set up a New Orleans touchdown.

"This was a real tough one," Peterson said. "I felt they didn't win the game, but rather we lost it. You can't turn the ball over like that and expect to win."

Drew Brees passed for just 197 yards but three touchdowns, a 38-yarder to Pierre Thomas, a 9-yarder to Devery Henderson, and a 5-yarder to Reggie Bush. Thomas added a 9-yard touchdown run as part of a 99-yard day rushing and receiving.

Most importantly, New Orleans turned the ball over only once—when Bush fumbled a punt inside the 10. But Peterson fumbled the ball back moments later to negate the miscue. "I know this; we came up with the turnover margin pretty significantly," Payton said. "So credit Minnesota at five-to-one and we win by a field goal. That's unusual."

The Saints had beaten two straight Super Bowl–winning quarterbacks (Favre and Arizona's Kurt Warner), but would have to knock off a third—Indianapolis' Peyton Manning—to secure their first NFL championship. The two weeks prior to Super Bowl XLIV would be a time of intense preparation for the New Orleans team, which found itself entering uncharted territory after years as the league's laughingstock.

But no one was looking that far ahead in the hours following the victory over Minnesota, when the celebrations all over Saints country went deep into the night. Perhaps longtime Saints radio play-by-play man Jim Henderson said it best, as Hartley's game-winner sailed through the uprights.

"Pigs have flown! Hell has frozen over! And the Saints are on their way to the Super Bowl!" ❧

NEW ORLEANS SAINTS VS. MINNESOTA VIKINGS						
	1	2	3	4	OT	FINAL
Minnesota	14	0	7	7	0	28 Record: (13–5)
New Orleans	7	7	7	7	3	31 Record: (15–3)

THE CONFETTI RAN SO DEEP ON THE SUPERDOME FIELD THAT JUBILANT SAINTS PLAYERS COULDN'T HELP BUT MAKE "CONFETTI ANGELS" AS THEY CELEBRATED THE TEAM'S FIRST-EVER TRIP TO THE SUPER BOWL.

GARRETT HARTLEY
CONNECTS ON THE FIELD
GOAL THAT INSTANTLY
SURPASSED TOM
DEMPSEY'S 63-YARD
EFFORT TO BECOME THE
MOST CELEBRATED KICK
IN FRANCHISE HISTORY.
THE 40-YARD BOOT WAS
GOOD AS SOON AS IT LEFT
HARTLEY'S FOOT, SENDING
THE SUPERDOME INTO
JUBLIATION.

Saints' "Cool" Brees Synonymous with New Orleans

It might not be much of an exaggeration to say that Drew Brees could one day run for mayor of New Orleans, and win. Such is his popularity in the Crescent City, where he has become an institution in just four years as the Saints' quarterback. The Texas native has become as identifiable with New Orleans as any local landmark or custom, wide receiver Devery Henderson told *The Sporting News* in January.

"He's a big deal," Henderson said. "When you think of Louisiana, people automatically think of down South,' maybe Cajun stuff and all that. And here in New Orleans you may think of Mardi Gras, the French Quarter, and the New Orleans Saints and Drew Brees."

Indeed, Brees' No. 9 jersey is the clothing of choice for thousands of Saints fans every Sunday, with only Reggie Bush's No. 25 approaching it in sales or popularity. But as loved and admired as Brees is by New Orleans in general, the feeling is mutual.

Brees fell in love with the area at an unusual time, signing with the Saints just six months after Hurricane Katrina had ravaged the entire Gulf Coast. But he saw past the flooded-out buildings and empty lots to something deeper, choosing New Orleans after being cast aside by the San Diego Chargers following the 2005 season.

"I tried to look a lot deeper than just on the surface," Brees said. "Coming to a team that had struggled a little bit coming on off a 3–13 season.… You're looking around at a lot of the neighborhoods and there are still boats in living rooms and trucks flipped upside down on top of houses—some houses just off the foundation and totally gone. You just say, 'man, what happened here?' It looks like a nuclear bomb went off. For me, I looked at that as an opportunity—an opportunity to be part of the rebuilding process. How many people get that opportunity in their life to be a part of something like that?

"The guys here, they looked me dead in the eye and said you're the guy to lead this team. You're the guy to lead us to a championship. We believe in you as much as you believe in yourself, and that meant a lot."

Brees made his mark immediately, passing for 4,418 yards and 26 touchdowns as New Orleans went 10–6 and advanced to the NFC Championship Game. He hasn't stopped throwing since, topping the 4,000-yard mark in each of his four seasons with the Saints, including an eye-popping 5,069 yards in 2008, the second-highest total in NFL history.

Brees was named *Sporting News* NFL Player of the

Drew Brees had the numbers and personal hardware of a champion thanks to an amazing career but lacked the team trophies his efforts deserved. The George Halas Trophy was the first step of two for Brees to take in 2009—the second was to come in Miami in the Super Bowl.

Year in 2008, and repeated the honor in 2009, when he passed for 4,388 yards, tied a career-high, and led the league with 34 touchdown passes and completed a personal-best 70.6 percent of his passes. He also led the league with a career-high 109.8 quarterback rating, earning a fourth trip to the Pro Bowl (though he had to decline the honor after the Saints made it to the Super Bowl).

"He's someone that does a great job with his own expectation level," said Saints coach Sean Payton, himself a former quarterback. "He's his own hardest critic, and in each offseason leading into the following year, he does a great job of looking closely at things he can do better. When you look at the type of season that he has had—not just statistically—but the job description for that position is to win, and he has been able to do that.

"And then when you look at his efficiency with throws underneath, his throws down the field, the touchdowns-to-interceptions; all those things he has been consistently better at and it starts with where he sets his sights and how high his standards are."

Brees, who turned 31 during the Saints' playoff bye week, got off to a red-hot start to the season, throwing for six touchdown passes in the season-opener against Detroit and three more in a Week 2 win over Philadelphia. He would go on to throw four touchdown passes against the New York Giants and five against New England, and threw three touchdowns against both Arizona and Minnesota in the playoffs.

What sets Brees apart is his accuracy, which is arguably as good as any quarterback to ever play the game. He makes up for less-than-ideal size (6-feet tall and a shade over 200 pounds) with textbook mechanics and fundamentals.

"That's an impressive guy, a very impressive guy," Eagles coach Andy Reid said. "It doesn't surprise me what he's done over the years here. He's a heck of a player. He looks as good as anybody in this league. My hat's off to him." ‿

BREES RALLIES HIS TEAM WITH HIS FAMOUS PREGAME CHANT. ONE OF THE BEST CAPTAINS IN THE NFL, HE LEADS HIS TEAM WITH AN UNDERSTATED FIRE THAT IS RARELY SEEN AMONG PRO QUARTERBACKS.

NEW ORLEANS SAINTS OWNER TOM BENSON HOLDS THE GEORGE HALAS
TROPHY AFTER THE SAINTS WON THEIR FIRST TRIP TO THE SUPER BOWL.